MW00628459

SPIRIT

SPIRIT

The Gift That Connects You to Heaven

DAVID BUTLER

DESERET
BOOK

Salt Lake City, Utah

To Emily—who loves and heeds the Spirit
more than anyone I know

© 2020 David Butler

All rights reserved. No part of this book may be reproduced in any form or by any means without permission in writing from the publisher, Deseret Book Company, at permissions@deseretbook.com or PO Box 30178, Salt Lake City, Utah 84130. This work is not an official publication of The Church of Jesus Christ of Latter-day Saints. The views expressed herein are the responsibility of the author and do not necessarily represent the position of the Church or of Deseret Book Company.

DESERET BOOK is a registered trademark of Deseret Book Company.

Visit us at deseretbook.com

Library of Congress Cataloging-in-Publication Data

Names: Butler, David (Seminary teacher), author.
Title: Spirit : the gift that connects you to heaven / David Butler.
Identifiers: LCCN 2020014854 | ISBN 9781629727783 (trade paperback)
Subjects: LCSH: The Church of Jesus Christ of Latter-day Saints—Doctrines. | Holy Spirit. | Gift of the Holy Ghost (Mormon theology) | Mormon Church—Doctrines.
Classification: LCC BX8643.H63 B88 2020 | DDC 231/.3—dc23
LC record available at https://lccn.loc.gov/2020014854

Printed in the United States of America
LSC Communications, Crawfordsville, IN

10 9 8 7 6 5 4 3 2

INTRODUCTION

Just so you know—I am a movies guy. I love movies. If it is ten minutes to midnight and I have to wake up for work the next morning at 5:00 a.m. and you invite me to go to the middle-of-the-night opening showing—I'm all in! I can't say no. It's not in my DNA. (But only under the condition that we are there for the previews—they are my favorite part!)

I like watching movies in the theater, movies on the basement couch, movies on the plane, movies on my phone, movies with a fox, in a box, and with green eggs and ham. I legit love movies. There is no chance I could tell you my favorite one, because it changes on the daily, but if you are looking for a good one for tonight, I am going to recommend *Field of Dreams*. I cry every time I watch it. It has stayed in my top-five favorite movies for a hundred years.

I am not sure how many total hours I have logged with Hollywood, but enough to be a bona fide movie expert. I know what makes a movie good. So with that claim, I will tell you that THE BEST MOVIES EVER MADE ARE THE ONES THAT SHOW A HERO'S JOURNEY. And not just an adventure type of journey (although those are the easiest to stay awake for during those midnight showings), but a journey that leads the hero through struggles and changes and overcoming. Where the heroes learn something about themselves (or they are reminded: "Simba . . . remember who you are"). Where they become someone new—someone better. These are the blockbuster hits. The movies that really speak to the soul! The classics.

I think one of the reasons I like movies like that is because they show me what can happen in an entire lifetime in just two hours (or like nine hours if it's a good trilogy). These stories resonate with us—they echo on our insides—because that's why each of us is here on earth. ------------>

We are here on a journey.
A journey that travels through struggles and changes and overcoming and eventually ends in victory.
THE VICTORY OF BECOMING.

But, oh man, it can be tough. Tough is PART of THE PROGRAM. And unfortunately, we don't get to speed through the hard parts with one of those three-minute inspirational songs that show the main character in the movie training and falling down and failing and getting back up again and waking up early and all of that until the person is ready for whatever the challenge is (you know what I'm talking about??). We have to live it. Every minute of it. Or some of the wise among us might say—we *get* to live it.

President Russell M. Nelson, one of those wise ones, stood up at his first general conference after being sustained the new prophet and President of the Church and said this goose-bump-giving line about the journey: "Our Savior and Redeemer, Jesus Christ, will perform some of His mightiest works between now and when He comes again. We will see miraculous indications that God the Father and His Son, Jesus Christ, preside over this Church in majesty and glory."

When I first heard him say that, I let out a little, "Believe that! Come on with that glory and majesty! What a day to be alive!" Then he kept going . . .

"BUT IN COMING DAYS, IT WILL NOT BE POSSIBLE TO **SURVIVE SPIRITUALLY** WITHOUT THE GUIDING, DIRECTING, COMFORTING, AND CONSTANT INFLUENCE OF THE **HOLY GHOST**."[1]

That one made me look over at the people I was watching with. What?? Wait. What's that mean? *Survival?* Go back and do that first line again. The glory one. I liked that one. It made me cheer. The second one scared me. But, actually, the more I have thought about it, I've realized this second line should make me cheer too. Cheer that we have a prophet who is seeing or sensing something coming and teaching us how to come out in glorious victory. And then cheer even louder that through this journey we are on—this one of overcoming and becoming—WE DO NOT HAVE TO DO IT ALONE. Like every hero in every good movie, we have a loyal companion by our side. We have

→ a Helper,

A MENTOR,

AND A FRIEND

who will guide, direct, and comfort. We have the promise and privilege of the constant influence of the Holy Ghost.

President Nelson isn't the only one to make this sort of promise. In fact, he was echoing Jesus Christ's words from nearly two thousand years ago. Picture Jesus sitting with His eleven closest disciples. (Judas, the betrayer, had already bailed by this time, the money bag he traded those majestic opportunities for dangling from his belt.) They had just enjoyed a wonderful dinner—the food most certainly was good, but the conversation is what got the five-star rating. They were all gathered together for what many of them didn't know would be their last supper as a team with Jesus.

It had been the best three years. They had witnessed mighty works and miraculous indications that He was the very Son of God living among them.

But then the conversation turned—from good to gulps—like in President Nelson's talk. Jesus told them the world was going to hate them and persecute them like it did Him. That rulers would kick them out of the churches and some of them would be killed. And then, after all of that, this kicker—Jesus told them, "And . . . I am leaving you." Well, that went sour pretty quickly. There must have been a silent pause, because Jesus then said, "None of you asketh me, Whither goest thou?" (John 16:5) That is a natural question when someone says he is leaving, right? Especially on the eve of super hard times. "Wait! Where are you going?? We were okay with danger if we knew you were going to be there with us." But instead they just sat there—pretty shocked, I imagine—with sad eyes and sadder hearts. But then Jesus promised them this:

> "NEVERTHELESS I TELL YOU THE TRUTH; **IT IS EXPEDIENT** FOR YOU THAT I GO AWAY: FOR IF I GO NOT AWAY, **THE COMFORTER** WILL NOT COME UNTO YOU; BUT IF I DEPART, I WILL SEND HIM UNTO YOU" (JOHN 16:7).

I love that Jesus had to begin that line with, "I tell you the truth." Every time I read it, I imagine that Jesus said it because the disciples wouldn't believe what He was about to say. Do you ever start stories like that? The really good stories? For some reason, I have the craziest and most random things happen in my life—I think I attract crazy—and on the weekly I will text a friend to start a conversation with this line: You are never going to believe what just happened to me.

That is what I imagine Jesus had to do too. The truth He was teaching them would sound so absurd, they wouldn't believe Him. "It is expedient that I go." In other words: It's for your good that I go. It will be an advantage. This will be better for you. I'm doing you a favor. His reason?

↳ *Because when I go, the Holy Spirit will be able to dwell in your hearts.* ↲

I would like to say that if I had been invited to that dinner, I would have been the first to oppose. How can that be true?

HOW CAN HAVING THE HOLY SPIRIT IN MY HEART BE BETTER THAN HAVING JESUS BY MY SIDE?

That does not sound like a good trade. That is maybe why Jesus first said—*Listen, I promise you what I'm about to say is true.*

If you are like me and have a hard time believing that, you *have* to read the sequel to the Gospels (Matthew, Mark, Luke, and John). It is called the book of Acts, and it is a book worth reading—movie worthy for sure! Acts is a book about a time a lot like our day.

It shows us what it looks like to have the **Holy Spirit** in our **hearts** while Jesus lives in heaven.

When the Spirit comes, as the Lord promised (in Acts chapter 2), He comes literally like a WILDFIRE among the disciples—with the sound and fervor of a HURRICANE. Poured out and whipping through them without holding back. And that little group and church grows and changes and moves through miracle after miracle after miracle with the excitement of a cowboy on the back of a rodeo bull. Sick people healed by shadows, boys falling out of windows and then raised to life, kings and captains and critics converted, missionaries saved from mobs and seers from shipwrecks—dreams, visions, prison walls coming down with a tumble that could never have been expected. As you read you can almost hear the good Lord in heaven saying to His little eleven: *I told you I was telling the truth.*

But let me ask you a question. Does that type of living from the book of Acts describe your life? WOULD YOU RATHER HAVE THE HOLY GHOST IN YOUR HEART THAN JESUS BY YOUR SIDE? Would you use words like *wonder* and *majesty* and *amazing* to describe the work of the Holy Spirit on your Tuesday afternoons? Have the work and promises of the Almighty God and the Tender Redeemer through Their messenger of grace stopped in our time? Or become more diluted? I wrote this book to try to convince you (and me) that the answer to those questions can be an absolute and emphatic *yes* and *no.* Respectively. No to the part about the Holy Spirit being less powerful in our time. Yes to the part where the amazing and miraculous can be a part of our own life experiences. All because of the mission and majesty of the Holy Spirit. Talk of the Spirit can be so commonplace. Let's change that.

I WANT US TO STAND AND CHEER AT THE THOUGHT THAT GOD HAS GIVEN US THIS REMARKABLE GIFT.

Elder Neal A. Maxwell once said: "The gift of the Holy Ghost truly is one of the greatest blessings available to members of the Church. . . . needed in every age and dispensation but certainly no less in the commotion-filled last days of the last dispensation. They are likewise needed at every stage and in every situation of life. . . . Yet, for different reasons, many of us live far below, or are unaware of, our privileges!"[2] I have heard this before and it makes me wonder—DO I ACTUALLY THINK AND BELIEVE THE HOLY GHOST IS THE

GREATEST GIFT AND BLESSING GOD COULD GIVE IN MORTALITY? Or would I prefer an iPhone? The new one has those memojis. They are legit. And what does it mean to live beneath my privileges? What are the privileges? Better than FaceTime?

In one of those movies I really like—one of the trilogies, actually—there is a character who drives me nuts because of how drastically he lives so far beneath his privileges. In case you are not a movie person, I'll fill you in. J. R. R. Tolkien wrote one of the most famous books of all time, and it became the movie trilogy The Lord of the Rings. If you haven't seen it yet, it is time. It's about a hobbit man who is given the responsibility of traveling across the world to throw an evil-possessed ring into a raging, erupting volcano that is surrounded and guarded by an army of nasty orcs and an all-seeing eye of a wicked, half-dead sorcerer creature. IT'S AN IMPOSSIBLE TASK FOR THE LITTLE HOBBIT. Happily and luckily, though, he is accompanied by a fellowship of friends who help him with his task—three other hobbits, an axe-wielding dwarf, an elvish archer, two mighty soldiers, and a powerful wizard named Gandalf. You already know I love it because of the journey and the hero and that good stuff, but let me tell you why I didn't love it. The wizard. He is a magical, mystical, all-powerful wizard. He can do anything. Yet out of the whole group, he is the most unhelpful. Any time the group gets into trouble, all he does is hit their enemies with his wooden staff. It drove me bonkers. For hours I watched a man who had the power to turn people into frogs hit them with a stick instead. WHAT WAS HE DOING? Use your magic! Burn them up! And why were they walking everywhere?? He. Was. A. Wizard. They should fly or teleport to the volcano. The problem could've been solved in ten minutes instead of nine hours. I couldn't stand it.

Someday, one of you Lord of the Rings experts needs to tell me all the rules of wizards or whatever so I can feel better about the whole thing, but in the meantime, here is my point. I was frustrated watching the wizard because of what he had the power to do and experience, and he wasn't doing it. He was living beneath his privileges. Just like we do. Sometimes we are just like that wizard.

That movie is fake. But our lives and journeys aren't. AND THEY MATTER MORE THAN ANYTHING. At times they might seem as impossible as a commotion-filled, continent-crossing trip to a volcano. Perhaps we could say that life is not survivable on our own. We live in a time of increased confusion, depression, loneliness, anxiety, and evil. But you know what? I'm not sad about it. I mean, of course, I'm sad when others face hard things, but it doesn't scare me. And I don't demand sympathy for myself or my kids growing up in a world like this one. Elder Neil L. Andersen said recently to students at BYU,

"As evil increases in the world, there is a compensatory **spiritual power** for the righteous.

"As the world slides from its spiritual moorings, the Lord prepares the way for those who seek Him, offering them greater assurance, greater confirmation, and greater confidence in the spiritual direction they are traveling.

"The gift of the **Holy Ghost** becomes a brighter light in the emerging twilight."[3]

Did you notice the phrase "compensatory spiritual power?" That comes from the word *compensation*. A compensation is an extra gift or benefit to match a disadvantage. Because the world is getting harder and harder, God is pouring out more and more power to match and overcome it. ARE WE MAKING THE JOURNEY WITH OUR OWN STRENGTH? Are we hitting our problems with wooden staffs? Because we don't have to! Are we unaware of or not embracing our privileges? Heavenly privileges like guidance in the dark, direction in the day, comfort when we fall, and strength when we fight.

These are promises that God has been pouring out since the beginning of this dispensation. When seventeen-year-old Joseph Smith was praying in his log-cabin bedroom one night, he was privileged with a visit from an angel named Moroni. There he was—a normal seventeen-year-old kid, in his pajamas, praying for forgiveness, and God sends a compensatory angel. Moroni quoted to him a line from the Old Testament prophet Joel. Joel said:

"And it shall come to pass afterward, THAT I WILL POUR OUT MY SPIRIT UPON ALL FLESH; and your sons and your daughters shall prophesy, your old men shall dream dreams, your young men shall see visions: And also upon the servants and upon the handmaids in those days will I pour out my spirit. And I will shew wonders in the heavens and in the earth" (Joel 2:28–30).

Interestingly, that was the same scripture that Peter quoted in Acts 2, when the Spirit and His privileges came down with the rush and wonder of a hundred earthquakes. After quoting that to Joseph, Moroni told him that the scripture was not yet fulfilled but was about to be! (see JS—H 1:41). In case you need the kind of help I do with history and dates, that visit from Moroni was in 1823.

SO YOU AND I HAPPEN TO LIVE IN THE TIME
THAT MORONI SAID WAS "ABOUT TO BE"—A
TIME WHEN THE SPIRIT COULD AND WOULD BE
POURED OUT—BUCKETS FULL—ON EVERYONE.
YOUNG, OLD, WOMEN, AND MEN FROM EVERY
NATION AND WALK OF LIFE COULD EXPERIENCE
THE WONDERS OF THE SPIRIT.

I had a boy in my first year of teaching seminary who stayed after class one day to chat. He had become one of my favorites that year. He was more on the quiet and contemplative side, but also fun-loving, and every now and then we would just catch up on life in between classes—usually about school or basketball or whatever. This one day, though, when he walked up, I could tell right away this wasn't going to be a typical jab at my Houston Rockets or a vent about why the closing shift at his work was the worst. He told me with these sincere, tear-filled eyes, "I am not usually a dreamer— but the last few nights I HAVE HAD A DREAM . . ." I was glued in. He then told me about his dream, and the second he started talking about it a sweet spirit settled on the conversation like dew from heaven. I won't tell you all the details of the dream, but it was one that indicated clearly to this boy that the Lord knew exactly who he was and had a tender spot for him in His heart. When he was done, he asked, "So what do you think?" Immediately the prophecy of Joel came into my head, and I thought—MORONI WAS RIGHT. And so was Jesus.

On that day and hopefully every day since then, that boy was living a book of Acts kind of life. A life President Nelson was teaching about, that Joel prophesied about, and that Jesus anticipated and promised for us. A different kind of life—a privileged one.

A life connected to heaven through the Holy Spirit.

The purpose of this book is to help all of us discover and then be excited to live up to our privileges—gifts given from God.

Life is going to be lonely, sad, confusing, tough, and dangerous, but **God offers gifts** of the
companionship,
comfort,
counsel,
power,
protection,
and purification
that come through the ministry of the Holy Spirit.
To **not just survive,** but to **live a life of wonder,**
majesty, glory, amazement, and miracles.
A life that changes the world.

A kind of life so good, you would expect to see it only in the movies.

WHO IS THE HOLY SPIRIT?

A couple of months ago our family moved houses, and I absolutely hated it. Every part of it. I thought it sounded fun at first but then quickly realized how much adult thinking and doing it required, and I wanted to break up with the idea. Getting our house ready to sell, negotiating prices, signing all the contracts, insurance stuff, tax stuff, financial stuff—the worst. No one grow up! Ever! As bad as all the adulting was, the hardest part of it all for me was packing up and getting rid of things. It was an emotional roller coaster. One minute I was ready to burn down the whole house so I didn't have to look at all the junk we owned—*how in the world did we have that much stuff????*—and the next minute I found myself crying when we sold and got rid of our bike trailer that we hadn't used in three years. Listen—I am a sentimental collector of things. I can't help it. I WAS SO ATTACHED TO THAT TRAILER. WE HAD TONS OF MEMORIES TOGETHER. It was there for the laughter of all our babies down the canyon on bike rides, it overheard the best conversations as we walked through the neighborhood on Sunday afternoons, and it went right along with the kids pretending it was a make-believe space shuttle or pirate ship or runaway train flying down the driveway. As I was breaking it down and folding it up to put in the new owner's car I almost caught myself reminiscing with it, "Remember that one day . . ." Oh, I really loved that bike trailer. I stood in front of our house as the people drove away with it like I was sending a child off to war or something. And yes, I told the people some of the stories about it. And yes, I asked them to take good care of it in a subtle, semi-awkward, roundabout way. And yes, I really did cry when they pulled away.

It might be too late, but I don't want you to think I'm a crazy person. Because yes, I know, I know, that the trailer was just a trailer. It is just metal and tires and spokes. I get it. But it was sad to see it go for the same reason you cried at the end of *Toy Story 3*. Those were just plastic toys! So quit judging me! But I realized that the reason I was sad about it going was because of the memories I had with it. MEMORIES WITH PEOPLE. Human memories were connected to the trailer—and that is what I loved. You see, there are a lot of things that I own that I would tell you I love. I love my Hydro Flask. I love my phone. I love my blanket. You have things like that too. But even though you say you love these things, they are just things. You might love having them, and the memories associated with them, but you don't have a relationship with them. BECAUSE THEY ARE NOT PEOPLE. THEY HAVE NO FEELINGS. And even though I thought I saw our trailer crying when it left, it didn't. And it didn't love me or care about me. Not one bit. (Why is that so sad to type?)

Now what does this have to do with the Holy Ghost? Well, you are going to find out that there might be a lot of things we don't know about the Spirit, but there are valuable, golden truths that we *do* know. And the first and most important point I want to make about Him is simply that—He is a Him. Not an it. Not a thing, like my trailer.

⟹ The Holy Ghost is a person.

In the Doctrine and Covenants, Joseph Smith taught that "the Father has a body of flesh and bones as tangible as man's;

the Son also; but the Holy Ghost has not a body of flesh and bones, but is a *personage* of Spirit" (Doctrine and Covenants 130:22; emphasis added). AND PERSONAGES OR PERSONS HAVE SOULS. They have emotions and personalities, likes and dislikes. They feel and they hope and they experience life. They love and have relationships.

You may sometimes read in scripture or hear in conference or talks in sacrament meeting the Holy Ghost referred to as an "it"—and that's okay. Don't freak out or stand up to correct people in the middle of their talks. That's bad manners. Plus, when referring to the Holy Ghost's presence or influence, it would be correct to say "it." But for our sake together here, I want to make a specific point to say that no matter *how* people refer to Him, He is a Him.

⟹ And that means **you** can have a relationship with Him.

You can feel things about Him—and He has feelings about and can have a relationship with you.

The Holy Ghost is a spirit son of our Heavenly Father. Technically, that would make Him one of your brothers. But He is more than a brother.

> HE IS ALSO A MEMBER
> OF THE GODHEAD.

Which means He is a God. Take a look at this teaching from the Prophet Joseph Smith—I don't understand all of it—but it is sort of mind blowing:

"An everlasting covenant was made between three personages

before the organization of this earth and relates to their dispensation of things to men on the earth. These personages . . . are called

{ GOD THE **FIRST,** THE CREATOR;
GOD THE **SECOND,** THE REDEEMER;
AND GOD THE **THIRD,** THE WITNESS
OR TESTATOR."[4] }

Joseph taught that while the Holy Ghost is subordinate to or under the direction of the Father, He still holds the keys of power, together with the other members of the Godhead. Again, that sounds super fancy and I don't know everything that it means, but what it does make clear to me is that

the **Holy Ghost** is not just a feeling in space or just a little messenger boy for God. He is **God the Third.**

We don't know very much about how He became who He is or what happened before this life—kind of like how we don't know very much about the past of God the Father, Jesus, or ourselves, either. We also don't know too much about His future. As a teacher, I often get asked whether the Holy Ghost will ever get a body. There is one source I know of from a man's journal in Nauvoo who recorded that Joseph Smith said that He is "waiting to take Himself a body."[5] So take that for what it is worth—a secondhand overhearing of Joseph Smith. There simply isn't very much recorded about where He came from or what His destiny is. We just don't know. BUT WHAT WE DO KNOW IS WHO HE IS TODAY.

And who is He? While reading scripture, it is often hard to know which member of the Godhead is being talked about. Sometimes it is pretty clear, but other times you may wonder after reading a verse about "God" or "the Lord" which one of the three it is. For example, when Nephi wants to see the vision of the tree of life that his dad Lehi saw, he not only gets to see the vision but gets a few tour guides through it. One of his personal tour guides is "the Spirit of the Lord," and Nephi said that "he spake unto me as a man speaketh with another" (1 Nephi 11:11). This easily could have been the spirit of Jehovah (Jesus), right? Or even the Father. However, in this case, if you read through the whole Book of Mormon, you would see that THE TITLE "SPIRIT OF THE LORD" iS USUALLY REFERRING TO THE HOLY GHOST, so it is probably Him—but we just can't know for sure. And that's okay.

ONE OF THE REASONS IT IS SO HARD IN CERTAIN SPOTS TO TELL **WHO IS WHO** IS BECAUSE OF HOW SIMILAR ALL THREE OF THEM ARE TO EACH OTHER.

In fact, They are so similar that in every book of scripture you find a verse like this one in 3 Nephi, when the Savior Himself says to the people, "Verily I say unto you, that the Father, and the Son, and the Holy Ghost are one; and I am in the Father, and the Father in me, and the Father and I are one" (3 Nephi 11:27).

Perhaps we could say that the Father, Son, and Holy Ghost are infinitely more ONE than They are separate. They absolutely are three distinct people, and if you stood in Their presence there would be four of you there, but as Elder Jeffrey R. Holland taught, "Having made the point of Their separate and distinct physical nature, we declare unequivocally that They were indeed and are 'one' in every other conceivable way—in mind and deed, in will and wish and hope, in faith and purpose and intent and love."[6] Think about those words Elder Holland used for a minute. Every other conceivable way! They are one in Their mind—in how They think and respond—as well as in Their wishes and hopes and intentions for you and me. And I also love that They are one in purpose, intent, and love.

They **all three** love us fiercely and all want what is best for us. All of Their intentions are the same— and those intentions are **so, so good.**

The Holy Ghost is perhaps the most misunderstood member of the Godhead, but by understanding how similar He is to the Father and the Son, we realize that we know a lot more about Him than we may have first thought.

For example, I was thinking the other day that I have never in all my years of church ever heard someone say,

"The Holy Ghost loves you."

It even sounds a little funny to hear. But why is it funny? It is true! HE DOES! He loves us with the same love of the Father and the Son. Maybe one of the reasons this idea is a little foreign to us is because of the titles we use for members of the Godhead. When we talk about God the First, we use the title of Father. When we talk about Jesus, we either use His name or a title like *Son* or *Savior*. Those are all "people titles." THEY ARE WORDS THAT DESCRIBE A RELATIONSHIP. I know how to love a father, love as a father, and feel the love of a father. I know how to love a son and how to be a son. No one really knows how to be or to love a ghost. It is a title that doesn't sound very cuddly. It frankly is kind of creepy. But the title of *ghost* or *spirit* is a description of His *physical* being—not of His personality. He is a person, which means He *has* a personality and emotions just like you and me. And more significantly, just like the other members of the Godhead.

I have always loved this quote from Heber C. Kimball. He said, "I am perfectly satisfied that my Father and my God is a cheerful, pleasant, lively, and good-natured Being. Why? Because I am cheerful, pleasant, lively, and good-natured when I have His Spirit."[7]

> # THE HOLY GHOST IS KIND, GENTLE, WONDERFUL, AND SENSITIVE, JUST LIKE THE FATHER AND THE SON ARE.

He gets happy and sometimes offended. He is proud of us in some moments and sad for us in others. He mourns, has a sense of humor, and laughs and has memories and interests. Just like They do. And His number-one interest happens to be you. At the end of a conversation I had with one of my own favorite people, Spencey, about the Holy Ghost and who He is and everything He does and wants to do for and with us, he said, "Wow, I have never thought about it like that before—the Spirit really is a someone. And not just any someone—the perfect friend. Someone you can love and feel love from." Yep—He is! That is what I want all of us to realize.

HE IS NOT A POWER, BUT A PERSON.

I am pretty sure you are catching my emphasis on how the Holy Ghost is a living being, but there is a difference between the power of the Holy Ghost and the actual personage of the Holy Ghost. THERE IS A DIFFERENCE BETWEEN **WHO** HE IS AND **WHAT** HE DOES. A past prophet, Joseph Fielding Smith, once said, "As a spirit personage the Holy Ghost has size and dimensions. He does not fill the immensity of space [as does the Light of Christ or the Spirit of Jesus Christ], and cannot be everywhere present in person at the same time."[8] That means He can only be in one place at one time, but HIS POWER AND INFLUENCE CAN BE FELT EVERYWHERE AND ANYWHERE THROUGHOUT THE WORLD. Technically, you could refer to that power as an "it." He is only in one place, but His power and influence can be experienced all over. He can be inspiring an artist in Japan and comforting a young mom in Kentucky all at the same time. Throughout this book, when I refer to the Holy Ghost being near us or watching over us or comforting us or other phrases like that, I am not implying that His personage is actually right there with you every single time. He could be. And for all intents and purposes, He might as well be. But since His influence can feel the same whether He is two feet away or two million miles away, most of the time we just don't know if He is *actually*, physically, right there.

In addition to His presence and influence, there is also a higher privilege that comes from the Holy Ghost called the gift of the Holy Ghost. Any person in the world may always have the guidance of God and frequent witnesses from the Holy Ghost, but the gift of the Holy Ghost is a higher gift of power that comes after a person is baptized and confirmed by proper priesthood authority.

It is not automatically there for all people—it is a **special gift** offered freely, but only given to those **who want** it and receive it by first receiving ordinances.

As you talk with and meet and become friends with people of other faiths, you might begin to wonder what the difference is between someone having the gift of the Holy Ghost and someone feeling the influence and power of the Holy Ghost. That is a hard question to answer. Other people who do not currently have the gift of the Holy Ghost are most definitely LED, GUIDED, INFLUENCED, LOVED, PROTECTED, AND STRENGTHENED. We see examples of that everywhere. And receiving the ordinances does not automatically mean we have received His influence and power into our lives. But it seems as if the difference that could exist with the gift of the Holy Ghost is having a more constant, consistent, and intense influence and power from the Holy Ghost in our lives. The Holy Ghost can reach ALL PEOPLE in the world, but every privilege we talk about in this book can come with greater INTENSITY and CONSISTENCY to those who have the blessing of the GIFT OF THE HOLY GHOST.

Now that was a lot of information! Let's do a quick summary.

THE **HOLY GHOST**: A PERSONAL BEING—THE THIRD MEMBER OF THE GODHEAD.

THE **POWER** OF THE **HOLY GHOST**: HIS INFLUENCE AND POWER FELT THROUGHOUT THE WORLD.

THE **GIFT** OF THE **HOLY GHOST**: THE BLESSINGS OF CONSISTENT AND MORE INTENSE EXPERIENCE WITH THE PERSON AND POWER OF THE HOLY GHOST.

If you want, you can go back over and read through those paragraphs again. If you want even more, I would also suggest looking up the terms in the Bible Dictionary, *True to the Faith*, and *Preach My Gospel* if you want to clarify or come up with some more questions. They have been so helpful to me. However, let me tell you a little something about trying to learn more about the Holy Ghost.

I have no idea (and I don't think anyone else on earth does either) how these things work. YOU CAN'T FIND THE ELEMENT FOR THE POWER OF GOD ON A PERIODIC TABLE. And how does it fill the immensity of space? And how does the Holy Ghost work and move through it to reach people all over the world?? No clue. And do we know when the Holy Ghost is influencing us personally or we are being influenced through His power or the Light of Christ? I don't think so. Not always, at least. Can He stand right near us? Sure. But do we know when it is Him or when it is an angel or when we are sensing the influence of the Godhead? Probably not. These things are hard (and sometimes impossible) to pin down with complete certainty. There is definitely some DIVINE MYSTERY to all of it. AND THAT'S OKAY! I think it makes it more intriguing and exciting. It seems more divine. There are a lot of things we don't understand. I have no clue how FaceTime works. None. How on earth does AT&T figure out how to get my face onto my friend's phone when he is in San Antonio, Texas, and I am in Honolulu, Hawaii? Somehow texts we send fly into space and then fly back onto someone else's phone. Magic. It's unexplainable to most of us. But somehow, it is working! And thank goodness! Because if I couldn't send GIFs, then what is life?? If people can find a way to get the Astros game into my house via light beams through the air, then certainly God can figure all of this out too, right? It's okay to say about the influence of the Light of Christ, the Holy Ghost, and gift of the Holy Ghost,

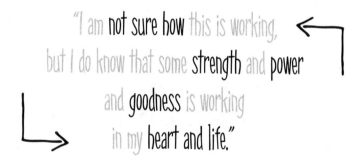

"I am not sure how this is working, but I do know that some strength and power and goodness is working in my heart and life."

So try not to get caught up in all the extras, and just enjoy the experience. The details aren't as important as the divine influence we can enjoy and *are* enjoying.

Having said that, one thing I for sure don't want to happen is for us to fall in love with the powers and gifts and experiences of the Holy Ghost and forget that they are coming through and because of a person. There are people I love that could give me the greatest and best gifts and I would not ever love those gifts more than I love the person who gave them. Ten for ten, I take the person over the gift. The greatest gift of the Holy Ghost is Him—the presence of the Giver Himself.

And what is He doing all day, every day? How is He using His power and influence? WHY IS HE GIVING GIFTS? Remember when the Lord said, "This is my work and my glory—to bring to pass the immortality and eternal life of man" (Moses 1:39)? The Holy Ghost, alongside the Father and the Son, will use all of His gifts, power, and presence to do the work that He wants to do. And that work is you—YOUR IMMORTALITY (living forever in a glorified body) and YOUR ETERNAL LIFE (your happiness and redemption).

Even though all members of the Godhead are unitedly working to bring about that one purpose, They each play unique roles in bringing it about. Only the Father is the father of us all and the source of all power and light and strength in the universe. Only the Son, Jesus Christ, suffered and died for our sins.

AND THE HOLY SPIRIT, AS JESUS PROMISED, WILL BE WITH US ON OUR JOURNEYS. RIGHT NEXT TO US IF WE WANT HIM TO BE.

There will be days we need a COMFORTER. There will be others when we will long for a TESTIFIER or a WITNESS. There will be days when we feel like we aren't enough and need a SANCTIFIER, a MAGNIFIER, or a GUIDE. Throughout this book, we are going to look at some of these roles He plays on the days we need Him most. What *are* those privileges of having Him near? He is and has always been in the work of calming, counseling, comforting, testifying, sanctifying, and exalting the family of God. Members of *His* family. A family He loves and cares deeply about—more than any*thing* in the world.

HOW TO RECOGNIZE
THE HOLY GHOST

Once upon a time, in a true story that goes something like this, President Boyd K. Packer was on a Church assignment in Germany to organize a stake in a place where Adolf Hitler once had a headquarters. The Hitler part is an unneeded detail, but I love the irony of it so much I had to include it. It was time for a new kind of king and kingdom in that place—time for miracles to replace misery. Anyway, after the stake conference, Elder Packer needed to take a train to another place in Germany. Two missionaries helped him and his wife get their tickets and get all situated on the right train. Just as it was pulling away, ONE OF THE MISSIONARIES HAD A THOUGHT and yelled up to Elder Packer, "Wait, do you have any German money?" He shook his head, so the missionary ran alongside the train, dug into his pocket, and handed Elder Packer a twenty-mark note through the window, and away they went. This was during a sketchy time in history, when feelings in East Germany were not as happy as they are today, and at two in the morning a large, burly soldier came into the Packers' train compartment demanding their tickets and passports. After looking through the passports, the military man started to talk angrily toward them in German. He kept leaving and coming back and yelling in more German. (Why does yelling in German sound so much scarier than in other languages??) Soon the Packers figured out that they had new regulations and there was a problem with Sister Packer's passport. NOT KNOWING WHAT TO DO, SUDDENLY A THOUGHT CAME TO ELDER PACKER'S MIND. He remembered the twenty-mark note from the missionary and handed it to the grumpy man. The man looked at it for a second, snatched it from Elder Packer's hands, handed back the passports, and moved on. Elder Packer didn't think much of it until he got to Berlin and told the story to the Church member who picked them up from the train station. The man got somber real quick and explained to them how dangerous of a situation they had actually been in. He was shocked and surprised that they hadn't been arrested, put in jail, or kicked off the train in the middle of the night somewhere in a scary neighborhood in East Germany—with no money, no cell phones, and no way of knowing what to do. IT WAS A MIRACLE THE SOLDIERS HAD LET THEM STAY on the train.[9]

Even though the yelling German captain is the most *dramatic* part of the story, the most *interesting* part of this story for me is from the perspective of the missionary.

When President Packer **remembered** the story, he **recognized** the guidance and direction and help of **the Spirit.**

Surely the missionary had been prompted to give him that money so the Packers wouldn't have to hitchhike through East Germany. BUT WHAT DOES THE MISSIONARY'S SIDE OF THE STORY LOOK LIKE? We don't know for sure, but you can imagine that when the missionary got home to his apartment that night, he could've written something like this in his journal: "Got to meet Elder Packer of the Quorum of the Twelve and his wife today. What a powerful couple. Funny thing happened, though. Just as his train was pulling away from the station, I had a thought to give him some of my German money. So I ran alongside the train like they do in the movies and handed him the money up through the window. I wonder why that happened. WAS THAT MY OWN THOUGHT OR WAS iT THE SPiRiT? Hope I have enough money for food next week."

So was it the missionary's own thoughts, or was it the Spirit? Hearing it from President Packer's point of view, the answer seems to be obvious—

YES, IT WAS THE SPIRIT. ⟸

But what about the missionary? All he saw was a train ride off from the station and a lighter wallet.

Most of the work and mission and ministry of the Holy Spirit in our lives happens inside our souls and is difficult to measure. It's invisible.

JUST BECAUSE WE CAN'T SEE SOMETHING DOESN'T MEAN IT ISN'T **REAL,**

but there are some CONFUSiNG parts of a relationship with someone who is iNViSiBLE!

And to complicate things, our thoughts, feelings, and emotions are also invisible, happen on the inside, and cannot be measured. It is no wonder we have a hard time distinguishing between EMOTiONS, THOUGHTS, and iMPRESSiONS and that we get confused about when and how the Spirit is interacting with us.

The most common question I have gotten as a teacher over the years is how to recognize whether some thought, feeling, nudge, impression, or inclination is coming from the Holy Ghost or from someone's own thoughts.

●●●

WAS THAT REALLY TRUE?
WAS THAT REALLY THE LORD?
HOW CAN I KNOW?

●●●

Sometimes we live our life story from President Packer's side, and we quickly get confirmation that some of those particular thoughts and impressions were from the Spirit. But, from my experience, most of the time I am on the side of the missionary—running alongside a train, digging money out of my pocket, and always wondering the same thing he probably did: IS THIS THE SPIRIT?

Lucky for us, in this story, we happen to know who that missionary was and what he learned from this experience. His name is Elder David A. Bednar, and he handed that money to President Packer about thirty years before they served in the Quorum of the Twelve together. Wild, huh? In a question-and-answer devotional I attended, someone asked Elder Bednar that age-old mystery—"How do we recognize the Holy Ghost in our lives and tell the difference between Him and our own thoughts?" I heard Elder Bednar tell that story about the train. He told us he DID wonder that day, and for many years after, if that had been his own thought or the Spirit. But then he taught us a truth he said he wished he had known earlier in life. And this is it:

You are making this too hard—it didn't matter.

It didn't matter? I thought. Doesn't it? Wouldn't that be

important to know? In another setting, he said something similar and taught that the problem is we usually overcomplicate the issue. He said simply,

"IF YOU HAVE A **THOUGHT** TO DO SOMETHING **GOOD,** IT'S **PROMPTED** BY THE HOLY GHOST."[10]

How about that for a short and sweet response to one of the most-asked questions in the Church? As we sit there and wonder, all we really need to do is to think to ourselves:

(If it is good, it comes from God)

That is going to be our first lesson in recognizing the Spirit. He is good. He is kind. And He is overly generous. Any thought that comes to our minds that is GOOD, KIND, or overly GENEROUS (or anything like that), we can know comes from Him.

Now, there are a lot of things that can make us feel good that are not from God. You might have someone in your math class that you think would feel really good to punch in the face. Or maybe you think looking at pornography will cause "good" feelings in your body. We cannot always trust our feelings. So what does Elder Bednar mean by "good"?

One of my favorite scriptures on what "good" means is in the Doctrine and Covenants. It is a revelation that came to Hyrum Smith, Joseph's big brother, when he wanted to know how he could help in the work. When Hyrum was anxious to get out spreading the good word, first the Lord told him to hold his horses for a minute because it wasn't quite time to go preaching, but in the waiting time there was something he could learn to do—trust in the Spirit. It is good to know that scriptural heroes like Hyrum also needed some training on how to trust the Spirit. "Verily, verily, I say unto thee, PUT YOUR TRUST IN THAT SPIRIT WHICH LEADETH TO DO GOOD—yea, to do justly, to walk humbly, to judge righteously; and this is my Spirit . . . , which shall enlighten your mind, which shall fill your soul with joy" (Doctrine and Covenants 11:12–13). These verses are a fantastic explanation of how to learn to trust if a feeling is the Spirit. The definition of "good." Take a look at some of the words. If a feeling comes from the Spirit, it will lead you to be just. *Just* means to be righteous—to have a conscience clear of offense toward God or other people. To be in a right relationship with God and others. It will make you feel humble. Humility is the opposite of pride. Pride is folding your arms, turning your back, and arguing with God. Will you have to argue with God after you do what you do? Will it make you more comfortable to turn your back and hide? If it is good, it can be done in front of God. The Lord told Hyrum the Spirit will also lead you to judge righteously—to ask yourself the question,

WHAT WOULD JESUS DO IN THIS MOMENT?

If you can picture Him doing it, then it is good. Moroni told us all how to judge in *this* way. He said, "Wherefore, all things which are good cometh of God; and that which is evil cometh of the devil; for the devil is an enemy unto God, and fighteth against him continually, and inviteth and enticeth to sin, and to do that which is evil continually. But behold, that which is of God inviteth and enticeth to do good continually; wherefore, every thing which inviteth and enticeth to do good, and to love God, and to serve him, is inspired of God" (Moroni 7:12–13).

Simple, right? All of these ways of living, the Lord said, will enlighten your mind and fill your soul with joy. Thinking of doing them will bring bright thoughts, and you will feel a closeness with the Lord and others. That is what it means to be and do good.

I have also always loved that the Lord's counsel to Hyrum was to *trust* in His Spirit. Meaning IT WAS GOING TO TAKE FAITH to do it. We only trust something when we don't know or can't see. If we know and can see for sure, it isn't called trust.

Did Elder Bednar know whether that thought was from the Spirit or not? No. But what if he took Doctrine and Covenants 11 as his guide? Was giving German money to a man traveling through Germany without German money a good thing? Absolutely. It ended up saving them from a midnight German excursion! But if the soldiers had never come, maybe Elder Packer could have just bought an ice cream when he got to Berlin. Win/win. Was it kind and nice and fair? Would Elder Bednar have to hide to do it? Pass it subtly behind the back like a drug deal? No. It was a GOOD thought. It was something he could imagine JESUS WOULD'VE DONE. And even if it *was* his own thought, God gets the glory. After all, at one time or another, God put the thought into Elder Bednar's mind—either while he was sitting in Primary, or in the car with his mom, or in the MTC—that helping other people is a good thing to do. No one EXCEPT THE SPIRIT knew what was going to happen on that train. And who knows how many years later Elder Bednar finally found out! But even if he never had found out, he could've walked away from the train station, feeling JOY for what he had done, and *trusting* that the Spirit was doing His work in and through all of them on that day.

The Holy Spirit is most definitely at work in all of our lives, and

As we have more and more EXPERIENCES, we become more CONFIDENT in RECOGNIZING His VOICE and FEELING His PRESENCE.

When I was growing up, everyone had home phones. For a while only the fanciest people had a service called "caller ID." Everyone has it now, but they had just started to make these phones that showed you the number that was calling so you would know who it was before you picked up the phone (or chose not to pick it up! Haha). It is wild to think how much answering the phone used to be a gamble back in the day! You never knew!! It could've been your crush or someone asking you to speak in church. Flip of the coin every time! So before caller ID was a common thing, on some Friday nights when my friends and I were bored with nothing else to do, a good time for me and my gang was prank calling people. When we get together now as more grown-up friends, we still laugh and laugh about some of those phone calls. One of my friends, Brent, loved to sit and listen to them, but hated doing it himself. He was way too nice and wasn't very good at fake accents and would always break character ten seconds into the call—so he couldn't do it. Also, he was a bad liar, and that was a good, good thing. It just made him bad at prank calling. Well, one night at like midnight, we finally convinced shy, meek, humble Brent to prank call someone. I told him,

"Just call and ask for John—that's all you have to do. I'll even dial the number." Usually we made up random phone numbers, but for Brent's first one I decided to call his parents' house. I'm a good friend. The phone rang and his dad picked up with a tired and groggy, "Hello?"

Then, Brent, "Hello, is John there?"

And then without any pause, his dad said, "Brent?"

And Brent said back in total surprise, "Dad!?"

We quickly hung up, and I am still laughing about it as I type this up.

Because the Spirit is a person, we relate to Him in some ways like we do everyone else. Brent's dad did not have caller ID, BUT THE SECOND HE HEARD HIS SON'S VOICE, HE KNEW WHO IT WAS. And the same was true for Brent about his dad. Think about your closest friends. Why and how are they your closest friends? Do you know what they are going to say before they say it? Would you recognize their voice without knowing who was calling?

We can have this same experience with the Spirit. After years and experiences trying to follow Him, learn from Him, and have Him move in us, we learn to know Him. We become more and more confident in recognizing when He is near. Nephi taught us that the Spirit speaks to us in a way we can understand: "For he speaketh unto men according to their language, unto their understanding" (2 Nephi 31:3). This doesn't just mean which language of the world we speak (although if you are German, He won't talk in Korean to you); it means

He speaks in ways that are familiar to you. ⟵

I can remember a day when the Spirit answered a significant prayer in my heart by reminding me of a clip from a movie. That's how He spoke to me. With a movie clip. He knows my language. And He knows yours. We have to remember that He is anxious to communicate with us. He wants us to learn how to recognize His presence.

Sometimes it is helpful to learn from other people the way they describe recognizing the Spirit. If you ask this question in a Primary class, you get the best answers. One time one of the kids in my Primary class said the feeling of the Spirit reminded her of marshmallows. Another one said, "Yeah, me too, but s'mores." (That kid was always trying to one-up everyone.)

{ *He will speak and will be recognized **differently** to different people in different situations.* }

Sometimes we hear the Spirit's presence described as a burning. The Lord said to Oliver Cowdery, "If it is right I will cause that your bosom shall burn within you" (Doctrine and Covenants 9:8). That is something that the Lord told Oliver Cowdery to help him understand translating the Book of Mormon. It was a specific revelation to him. It is not a scripture that means that is how the Holy Ghost will feel every time. Growing up, I was particularly confused by that because, first, I thought your bosom was your bum. For those of you who are like me, let me help you understand that your bosom is your chest. That would've been extremely helpful information for me twenty years ago. But more importantly, for a long time, I was bothered and worried that I didn't ever have a burning in my heart. President Dallin H. Oaks once said that burning is not an actual source of heat, but the feeling of "COMFORT AND SERENITY."[11] Once I started hearing other words describing the Spirit—words like PEACE, CONFIDENCE, DESIRE FOR GOOD, PATIENCE, and OPTIMISM—I started to recognize experiences I thought could be the Spirit. It is still a work in progress, but I was thrilled to know that I wasn't the only one in the room not being influenced by heaven through a burning. Another scripture that was helpful is Doctrine and Covenants 85:6: "Yea, thus saith the still small voice, which whispereth through and pierceth all things, and often times it maketh my bones to quake." Take a look at some of those words— *still*, *small*, *whisper*, *pierce* through anything, *quake*. In Israel, there is a mountain called Mount Horeb—or you may know it as Sinai. On this same mountain, two different prophets had their own experience with the Lord on two different occasions. For Elijah, the Lord sent a great and strong wind that caused a mini avalanche, an earthquake, and a fire. After each of these we learn that "the Lord was not in the fire [or earthquake or wind]: and after the fire a still small voice" (1 Kings 19:12). Funny enough, several years earlier, Moses was on the same mountain with a burning bush—fire!—and it *was* the Lord.

Elijah got a **whisper,** and Moses got a **flame.**

Sometimes the Spirit will manifest Himself differently to us. One of the best pieces of advice someone ever gave me when learning to recognize the Spirit was to ask God for help. ASK Him to help YOU LEARN THE WAY HE SPEAKS TO YOU. It will be a process, but remember that is exactly how He wants it. If it takes longer, that means a longer amount of time you spend together—and that is exactly what He would hope for.

You are not the only one learning and wondering your way through this. I love the story in the Gospel of Luke about John the Baptist sending a message to Jesus from jail. (I don't love that he was in jail, by the way.) We don't really know what was going through John's mind and heart, but Luke tells us that from his prison cell, John sent two of his friends to Jesus with a message from him asking, "Art thou he that should come? or look we for another?" (Luke 7:20). Do you love that that question came from John the Baptist? John—the one who stood in the river with Jesus and baptized Him while God spoke from the clouds and the sign of the Holy Ghost descended upon Him as a dove. *That* John, the preordained forerunner to Jesus, the one who leapt in his own mom's tummy when Mary came to visit—he sent friends to verify that Jesus really was the Messiah. ARE YOU REALLY HIM? When I read this story, it makes me feel good about the process of learning to recognize the Holy Spirit in my life.

If John had trouble recognizing who Jesus was—even after being together in the Jordan River—then it might take me **some time** to recognize an invisible member of the Godhead working in my life.

The Lord was okay with John needing time, and HE IS OKAY WITH US NEEDING TIME. Remember—it is just more time together! Jesus's answer also gives all of us some great advice: "Go your way, and tell John what things ye have seen and heard; how that the blind see, the lame walk, the lepers are cleansed, the deaf hear, the dead are raised, to the poor the gospel is preached" (Luke 7:22). He asks John, and all of us, to consider what is happening. What are we experiencing? Where is it leading? The Apostle Paul wrote once that when we try to "walk in the Spirit" (Galatians 5:16), we begin to recognize things changing in us. He called these changes "fruits." That is a great comparison, since fruits take a while to grow. I planted a peach tree in my backyard four years ago and just barely got my first peach. Paul said, "The fruit of the Spirit is love, joy, peace, longsuffering, gentleness, goodness, faith, meekness, temperance: against such there is no law" (Galatians 5:22–23). Over time, we will notice these feelings growing in us. They are the mark of a person living in companionship with the Spirit. THE WORK OF THE WHOLE GODHEAD WILL LEAD TO CHANGE, TO MIRACLES, AND TO GOOD. And those will either come as protection on a midnight train or ice cream in Berlin. But as we are learning to trust, the miracles will keep coming. The Spirit is going to continue working wonders in our lives even when we don't recognize Him there. So KEEP ASKING, and KEEP LISTENING, and BE PATIENT—all meaningful relationships take time.

✳ And this is a **relationship worth having**—a friend, ✳ a revealer, a helper, and a sanctifier—a member of the Godhead within whispering distance.

In the next chapters we will talk about why we want such a person so close, the different ways He hopes to interact with us, and what He is trying to do to help us through our journeys.

THE WITNESS

About a year after Jenny and I got married, we lived in the dumpiest little apartment. It kind of smelled like diseases, half of the electric plugs didn't work, and I thought the banister going up the stairs was going to bust off every time I held on to it. One of our first days there, the Relief Society president came over with a map of the neighborhood to show Jenny which streets she should avoid at night and which streets she should avoid all the time. All of this contributed to my overjoyed reaction when Jenny told me when I walked in after school one night that I got in.

"In where?" I asked.

"To BYU–Hawaii!" she squealed back!

Yahooooo! We were outta there! Goodbye, drug dealers. Adios, stinky bathroom. Peace out, moldy tile. And aloooooha, Hawaii!

LIVING IN HAWAII MIGHT BE ONE OF THE TOP THREE BEST DECISIONS WE HAVE EVER MADE IN OUR LIVES. It has been years since we have moved back, but I am still homesick for it. And often, usually while driving down the freeway in the snow, I wonder why I ever moved away from my little paradise place. Our "apartment" over there was a single bedroom in a house that we lived in with two other couples with about a fifth the living space of our previous one. We shared everything—the bathroom, the kitchen, the refrigerator (where one of the dude's leftovers always dripped out of his Styrofoam containers onto our milk). And our next-door neighbors legitimately sold drugs and raised roosters for cockfighting. One of the things we thought might be the hardest was living miles and miles away from our family and friends back home. Hawaii is a tiny island out in the middle of a gigantic sea. Who knows how sailors first discovered it! It is not an easy place to get to, and it is never convenient to leave. But despite all of this, I loved it!

I loved everything about it.

The smells, the sights, the experiences—all of it. Every memory from Hawaii is golden to me.

Jenny and I didn't live there super long, but there was something about it that really won my heart. The locals call it the Aloha Spirit. It's the phrase they use to describe why Hawaii seems so magical—why people are nicer and let you go first in traffic or why there is just a more relaxed and friendly vibe in the air. I'm not sure of the source, but ALOHA SPIRIT is a real thing. Maybe it is the beautiful setting. Or perhaps it is the way that people love so abundantly. Or maybe it is the mangoes. (That really could be it.) Whatever it is or wherever it comes from, and whether or not it is a thing for anyone else, Hawaii has a special spirit about it and has a unique spot in *my* heart because it was in that place, even though I was separated from home, that I felt like I was especially close and connected with God.

There were days when I would be floating out in the ocean between sets of waves and I would look up at the towering mountains cascading over the sandy beach where I had left my flip-flops and I would just get lost in the magic of it all. I couldn't help but feel so small compared to the majesty all around me—and yet, as insignificant as I seemed in such a big blue sea, I could sense a divine attention focused on my life, and a love from heaven that beat in me.

IT WAS DURING THOSE DAYS THAT I STARTED TO BELIEVE THAT GOD WAS REAL AND THAT HE AND I HAD AN ACTUAL CONNECTION. A CERTAINTY WAS BORN THERE NOT ONLY THAT HE LIVED, BUT THAT HE LIVED IN ME.

Jenny and I ended up naming our first son Jackson Kai. Jackson was after our favorite singer, who lived just down the road, but *Kai* was significant. It is the Hawaiian word for ocean. When my son grew up and asked about his name, I wanted to tell Jack about those feelings and experiences I had out in the ocean. I wanted to tell him how I was alone but felt close. Another word we considered for Jack's middle name was *Ha*. The sound "ha," which is part of the word *aloha*, is a Hawaiian word that means BREATH AND LIFE. It is a kind of life that is filled with spirit and love and vibrancy and majesty. It is what you "breathe" upon and wish upon people when you greet them with "Aloha" (usually accompanied with kisses on the cheek. I miss that about Hawaii too!).

Interestingly, in the very beginning book of Genesis in the Bible, the Creation of man is told with these words: "And the Lord God formed man of the dust of the ground, and breathed into his nostrils the breath of life; and man became a living soul" (Genesis 2:7).

Now, obviously this account is symbolic. God did not really give CPR to Adam and breathe into his nose to give him life, but I love the idea that each of us live because of the life that God breathed into us. One interpretation of these scriptures might be the description of Adam getting his premortal spirit put into him, but God puts another kind of spirit into us as well. His spirit.

IN SOME ANCIENT LANGUAGES, THE WORDS FOR BREATH AND SPIRIT ARE THE SAME WORD.

When I read the story, I imagine a scene right before God sends us away from heaven, where He breathes into us life, spirit, and love for our journey. Don't you sense it? This feeling of the LIFE, SPIRIT, and LOVE that we can and do feel from God the Father comes to us THROUGH THE HOLY SPIRIT. You might not ever get the chance to experience the Aloha Spirit in Hawaii, but you do get to experience the Spirit of God while you are here on this earth. You get to feel a connection with your heavenly home and with God while you are away.

Sometimes in our church world, we call this experience of connection with God "inspiration" or "revelation." These are such big and fancy words that we sometimes lose the wonder of what they actually are. One year as a seminary teacher, I wanted to test this out, and I asked my students to close their eyes and raise their hands if they ever felt they had received a revelation before. Only about a third of the class raised their hands. I asked them to put their hands down and then asked them to raise their hands if they thought they had ever felt the Holy Ghost. Nearly everyone in the class raised a hand. I put the two numbers up next to each other on the board and then asked, "What is wrong with these numbers?" It didn't take long for someone to say, "THE NUMBERS SHOULD BE THE SAME." Exactly! *Revelation* is a word that sometimes we might associate only with prophets and visions. In fact, I had a picture of the First Vision up on the screen behind me while I was asking the questions. I did that to make a point. When some people hear the word *revelation*, they think Joseph Smith, the Sacred Grove, the Doctrine and Covenants, the translations, angels, visits, and all the things. Yes, it can mean all those, but if the story of the First Vision taught us anything, it is that

GOD IS WILLING TO SPEAK AND CONNECT WITH **ANYONE**

—even fourteen-year-old farm boys. One simple definition I have given to myself is that revelation is a personal, one-on-one interaction with God. A moment when He reaches into our stories. It can be a SURGE OF CONFIDENCE or an ANSWER TO WHAT TO DO NEXT. It could be the RIGHT WORDS TO SAY or a FEELING THAT SOMETHING IS TRUE. These are all connections with God. They could all be called revelation.

They all come because of the **Holy Spirit.** He is the one who seems to **bring** revelation and inspiration (in all its forms) from the Father to His children. ------→ **He is who connects us.** ------→

I have said this before, but saying goodbye is one of my hardest things to do. I can't stand it. I live for relationships and connections with people—so when we split up it is a real doozy for me. I keep countdowns on my phone for when I will see people I like again, I always ask people to ride in the car with me if I'm driving somewhere, and I still cry when I leave my parents' home after a trip down in Texas. And going on my mission—oh, man—buckets of tears! The new change to allow missionaries to call or Skype home once a week is the best idea I heard all year. Why wasn't that around when I was a missionary?! I have no memory of this, but I am certain it took extra encouragement and tender nudging when I left the presence of our Heavenly Parents to come to earth. I can also imagine I reluctantly raised my hand to sustain any idea about a veil being placed over my memory. Sometimes I still feel homesick for heaven. But God knew what the separation would be like. In fact, Elder Ronald A. Rasband once taught, "Our Father in Heaven knew that in mortality we would face challenges, tribulation, and turmoil; He knew we would wrestle with questions, disappointments, temptations, and weaknesses. To give us mortal strength and divine guidance, He provided the Holy Spirit. . . . THE HOLY GHOST BINDS US TO THE LORD. By divine assignment, He inspires, testifies, teaches, and prompts us to walk in the light of the Lord."[12]

Do you love that line—"THE HOLY GHOST BINDS US TO THE LORD"? He keeps us connected with home—with Him. Right now, I don't live at my parents' house in Texas or anywhere near it. I know in my mind that my parents back at home love me. They have shown it to me again and again, and I am confident in saying that it is a fact. In fact, I will.

> DEAR WORLD:
> MY PARENTS LOVE ME!

See? But even though I know that is true in my mind, I am not currently feeling it in my heart. It is hard to show or feel that kind of love when you are not talking or seeing each other at that very moment. The memories are sweet, but the distance makes it difficult. I don't know where heaven is, but most likely, it is geographically farther away than Texas.

However, because of the Holy Ghost, ← I can be away from our Heavenly Parents and away from Jesus and still → feel Their love.

The Spirit has the power and privilege of taking information that I know is true in my head and helping me feel it in my heart. There is a difference between a little girl saying that she knows her dad loves her and the moment when he picks her up, kisses her on the cheek, twirls her around, and says it to her. These are the kind of moments the Holy Spirit provides.

Paul wrote in a letter to the Roman Saints, "For ye have not received the spirit of bondage again to fear; but ye have received the Spirit of adoption, whereby we cry, Abba, Father. The Spirit itself beareth witness with our spirit, that we are the children of God" (Romans 8:15–16). Those are tough verses to understand, but one thing they are teaching is that THE SPIRIT HELPS US take the fact in our head that GOD LOVES US and makes it come alive in our hearts— SPIRIT TO SPIRIT. That word *Abba* is a word that means father, but in a more tender and connected way—like "daddy." The Spirit carries that same feeling and tender connection with the Father into us. Gives us that twirl feeling. Because of the Holy Ghost, we no longer feel like simply creations of God, but now we sense in a real way that we are His children—His little boys and girls.

In that same chapter, Paul teaches, "Likewise the Spirit also helpeth our infirmities: for we know not what we should pray for as we ought: but the Spirit itself maketh intercession for us with groanings which cannot be uttered" (Romans 8:26). HAVE YOU EVER HAD A CONVERSATION WITH SOMEONE AND FELT LIKE YOU COULDN'T FIND THE RIGHT WORDS TO SAY? You're trying to explain something and it just isn't coming out right. It is so frustrating—especially when you are trying to explain the way that you feel. Like when a doctor asks you questions about some pain or sickness you are having and you can never explain it quite right. Is it more the upper arm or just the elbow? Is it a burning feeling or more of a sharp pain? How would you rate it on a scale of one to ten? It is so frustrating to try to explain some things—especially things that really matter! Because of the Spirit, we don't have conversations like this with the Lord. Even if we groan through them, as Paul taught, the Spirit helps us still feel understood and connected with Him—LIKE A FRIEND WHO JUST GETS IT. My first mission president when I got to Korea was Korean. He could understand English—I thought—and most of our conversations in the beginning were just smiles back and forth with each other and went something like this.

Him: Are you healthy?
Me: Yes (with my thumbs up as if he
    didn't understand the word "yes").
Him: Are you happy?
Me: Yes (again—thumbs up!).
Him: Good work, Elder! Keep it up!

You could say we weren't super close with each other after all of those riveting conversations. But during one of the first months of my mission, I needed to talk through some difficult situations with him. I TRIED SO HARD TO COMMUNICATE—flipping through my dictionary and fumbling through my words—probably swearing unknowingly or telling him I had a hippopotamus in my ankle. I wanted to be understood so badly. I finally just put the dictionary down on the desk, put my head down further, and gave up. Just then, he reached across the desk to grab my hand. I looked up in his eyes, and with a sweet conviction and confidence, he said, "I UNDERSTAND." I have felt the Holy Spirit do the same for me in prayer.

HIS INFLUENCE FEELS LIKE THE HAND OF THE FATHER, REACHING ACROSS TIME AND SPACE, GRABBING MY HAND, AND SAYING, "I UNDERSTAND."

In those same verses, it also seems like Paul is teaching that the Spirit will teach us *what* to pray for at times. There are some situations you find yourself in where you know you need help, but you just don't know what to ask for or if you should ask for it. The Spirit helps us through this too.

Even though God might be a billion miles away, the **Holy Ghost** makes it **feel like** He is sitting right next to us understanding everything in our **hearts** and living our lives with us side by side.

I felt this a few years ago when Jenny and I took our oldest kids over to the Cook Islands to visit Jenny's parents, who were serving there as missionaries. I must have a thing for islands, because our visit there was so life-giving. And they have great mangoes too! During the end of our visit, Jenny and I did a youth conference for all the youth and young adults that lived on the big island of Raratonga. During Jenny's talk, she said a line that I have not forgotten. Her best line! She said to those who were sitting in the little Polynesian chapel, "There is a lot of Jesus on this island." Amen! It is exactly how I felt all week. That is a line that I have thought about again and again, and even said under my breath in other places we have been. I love the line just as it is, but what it means is, "There is a lot of the Spirit and love of the Godhead in this place. We feel Their presence. We feel alive and connected to Them and to each other." THAT FEELING AND EXPERIENCE OF "A LOT OF JESUS" IS ACTUALLY THE WORK AND POWER OF THE HOLY SPIRIT. That is a powerful and beautiful gift. We are away from home with a veil over us, and yet we can still actually say that we feel Their presence in a small chapel out in the middle of the sea. This doesn't only happen on beautiful islands. I think being in God's creations helps us think of Him more—and that probably helps—but I have felt that connection with God in a stinky alleyway in Seoul, walking through a normal neighborhood in Dallas, Texas, and sitting on a curb on the side of the road. When the prophet Mormon wrote about the forest and the waters and area where all of Alma's people were baptized, he said, "How beautiful are they TO THE EYES of them who there came to the knowledge of their Redeemer" (Mosiah 18:30). Just moments before, Alma had prayed and asked the Lord to "pour out thy Spirit" (Mosiah 18:12). I think these ideas are connected, because the Spirit connected the people there to the Redeemer. And because of that, the place became beautiful.

ANY PLACE CAN
BECOME BEAUTIFUL,
AND BECAUSE OF THE HOLY SPIRIT, GOD CAN REACH US ANYWHERE.

The other week, I clicked on an article that popped up on Facebook about Buzz Aldrin, who was the second man to walk on the moon.[13] When Neil Armstrong and Buzz landed the Eagle lunar module on the moon, they had to wait for their bodies to adjust before they were allowed to step out onto the moon's surface. While they sat there and waited, Buzz Aldrin asked NASA for a moment of silence, and he prepared and partook of the holy sacrament.

Buzz Aldrin was an elder at his church, the Webster Presbyterian Church, and had received permission to take the bread and wine on their spaceship in order to be able to take the sacrament on the moon. He said, "I poured the wine into the chalice our church had given me. In the one-sixth gravity of the moon, the wine curled slowly and gracefully up the side of the cup." THE FIRST ITEMS EATEN ON THE MOON WERE THE SYMBOLS OF JESUS'S BODY AND BLOOD FOR ALL OF US. The scripture that Buzz then read and wrote down while sitting in the lunar module was from John 15, the setting of the Last Supper, when Jesus gave the sacrament to His disciples. "I am the vine, ye are the branches: He that abideth in me, and I in him, the same bringeth forth much fruit: for without me ye can do nothing" (John 15:5). We have already learned that the way we abide in Him or stay connected to Him like a branch to a vine is through the Holy Spirit. On that day, the moon became a beautiful place for Buzz Aldrin—and not just because it is the moon.

Each week in our church buildings on earth (whether they are pretty chapels or second-floor rented rooms), AS WE TAKE THE SACRAMENT in our own meetings, WE CAN FEEL THIS CONNECTION in a significant way.

We promise the Father that we will always remember His Son. He then promises to us in return that we may **always have His Spirit to be with us.** We then eat and drink those symbols **into** our bodies. We take Them in. The bread of life, the water of life, **the spirit of life.**

In that same letter to the Romans we were talking about earlier, Paul taught one of my most favorite truths about the Spirit to those Saints. It's another one of those goose-bump-giving lines for me. "And if Christ be in you, . . . the Spirit of him that raised up Jesus from the dead dwell in you" (Romans 8:10–11). This verse is a little tough to understand, but it is saying that the same power that raised Jesus from the grave on the third day can live in us. IT CAN GIVE US LIFE. You can walk into school on the first day or be shopping or driving down the road and have that same Spirit in you.

Wherever we are, or **whatever** we have done, we can be **within** that **whispering distance** of the Father, the Son, and the Holy Spirit.

We can be from the dust of the earth or we can be living in a stinky apartment. We can be in the middle of the sea or we can be as far away and alone as the moon. "For I am persuaded, that neither death, nor life, nor angels, nor principalities, nor powers, nor things present, nor things to come, Nor height, nor depth, nor any other creature, shall be able to separate us from the love of God, which is in Christ Jesus our Lord" (Romans 8:38–39). This is made possible because of the mission and ministry of the Spirit. He was specifically sent by the Father, by divine assignment, to MAKE SURE WE ALWAYS STAYED CONNECTED TO HOME—to bind us to the Father. To help us improve and continue to live out a relationship with the Father and the Son. To feel at home—that breath-of-life Aloha spirit—wherever our current place of residence may be or whatever it may look like.

⇒ THE TESTIFIER ⇐

When I was about fourteen, our family went on a cross-country road trip in an RV. We went from Texas to New York, across to Illinois, and then down to Texas again (with a hundred stops in between). We had taken road trips before, but this one took the cake. On all of the other ones, we crammed a million people into the Suburban for the most uncomfortable way to travel on earth. Having someone's foot in your face or a seat belt buckle jammed into your back for twenty-four hours is like ancient Chinese torture. RV TRAVELING, on the other hand (when you are not the driver),  iS THE BEST! We went everywhere! We saw a lot of Church history places like the Sacred Grove, Hill Cumorah (I got yelled at for rolling down it), the Independence temple lot, Liberty Jail, Nauvoo—all the things. We also crammed in the Baseball Hall of Fame, Football Hall of Fame, Washington, D.C., Liberty Bell in Philadelphia, a few nights on Broadway, and the crème de la crème—the Field of Dreams. That trip was over twenty years ago (I am now the driver for trips like that—lame!), and we did so many things. I left out a lot because I didn't want you to be jealous. But I gave you the big list to help you see how fast-paced the whole thing was. Even though we were moving from thing to thing to thing, and it was just one trip among many that I took as a kid with my family, for some reason, there are experiences on that particular vacation that are almost highlighted in my memory. They haven't faded. They left a deeper kind of impression on me—like GOD HAS LEFT A FINGERPRINT ON MY HEART.

One of those experiences that seems insignificant, but I still have in my mind with perfect memory, is visiting the Washington D.C. Temple. Before the trip, I don't think I even knew there was a Washington D.C. Temple. If you have been there before, you may know why local drivers call the stretch of road that passes it one of the most dangerous spots on the beltway. When we went it was nighttime, and as you drive closer, you pass through thick forest area with tons of trees. Then all of a sudden the temple pops up out from among the trees out of nowhere into the most spectacular sight—especially at nighttime. I have heard from my friend who lives there that the city asked the temple if they could turn down their lights because of the distraction the temple was causing drivers. I don't know if that story is true, but what is true is the temple is so bright and bold when you turn that corner that I am surprised more people don't Mario-Kart-style drive right off the road. When we got to the temple and walked around, we passed the most gigantic spotlights you have ever seen. They put the Batman signal spotlight to shame! Their job, as you know, is to light up the temple. And even though they are so impressive and powerful, no one ever really notices them or gives them credit. No one turns the corner on the beltway and says, "Wow! Look at that light! I bet the spotlights on that thing are like 20,000 watts! I wonder what those bulbs cost. Those must be amazing. Let's go take a look, kids!" Nope—that has never happened.

WHAT PEOPLE NOTICE IS THE TEMPLE. AND THEY NOTICE IT EVEN MORE BECAUSE OF THE LIGHTS. WHICH MEANS IF THE LIGHTS ARE DOING THEIR JOB, THEN NO ONE EVER NOTICES THEM—THEY ONLY NOTICE THE TEMPLE.

That is what the lights were put there to do—to make the temple sparkle.

When Jesus was at that famous Last Supper we have talked about a few times already, He told His disciples this truth about the Holy Ghost who would come. "But when the Comforter is come, whom I shall send unto you from the Father, even the Spirit of truth, . . . HE SHALL TESTIFY OF ME" (John 15:26). Nephi, on the other side of the world, said something similar: "And ye have received the Holy Ghost, WHICH WITNESSES OF THE FATHER AND THE SON" (2 Nephi 31:18). One of the reasons we probably don't know much or talk much about the Holy Ghost as a person is because He is doing His job.

And when He is **doing His job,** you don't walk away and think about **Him,** but you walk away **thinking more about the Father and the Son.**

All of His purpose is to try to point you away from Him and toward Them. To make Them sparkle.

Jesus told the disciples that "the Comforter, which is the Holy Ghost . . . shall teach you *all* things, and bring *all* things to your remembrance" (John 14:26; emphasis added).

> The Holy Ghost was also sent and has a responsibility to **witness and testify** to our hearts of all the things that are true.

Of all the truths that the Holy Spirit came to bear witness of or teach, the DIVINITY and LOVE and MAJESTY OF THE FATHER and the SON are at the top of the list.

There are a lot of ways people have to determine what is true. As much as you don't want to think about this (especially if you are reading this in the summer), the scientific method, for example, is a perfectly fantastic way to discover truths. I am so glad that people do experiments to figure things out. I would rather you find out that certain medicines work through the scientific method before you ever give them to me to use. A few years ago I had laser eye surgery done. I was happy to know that it had been tested and verified by millions of people before me. I knew it was a valid procedure. Bless the heart of the person who went first!

Even though we know we can learn truth by reason, testing, sight, hearing, and touch, we also have to remember that there are CERTAIN TRUTHS we learn in a way that DOESN'T USE OUR FIVE SENSES or a LAB ROOM. As a missionary, I would play the game twenty questions with families sometimes to teach them this. You've played, right? You think of something . . . like a tiger . . . and they have to ask you yes-or-no questions to try to figure out what it is. If they can do it before asking twenty questions, they win. "Is it an animal?" "Yes." "Does it live in the sea?" "Nope." Okay, you get it! After a normal round or two, I would choose the word *love*. When the questions came in, it got harder to answer and harder to guess. "Is it big?" "Ummmm. Yes. Very." "Is it alive?" "Sorta . . . yeah!" "Can you see it?" "No. Not it. But the effects of it." "Can you feel it?" "Absolutely!" "Is it real?" "Yes." "But you can't see it?" "That's right. And even though you already asked that, confirming it still counts as a question." It was almost impossible to answer with a simple yes or no. The families would go crazy trying to figure out what it was. When I was done, I would tell them it was love, and they would all let out a questioning and doubtful "Aaaaaaah" until they thought about it and realized I was right.

LOVE IS A REAL THING, BUT IT IS SO HARD TO DESCRIBE. IT IS ALSO ONE OF THE MOST POWERFUL FORCES ON EARTH—YET NO ONE CAN SEE IT, HEAR IT, OR MEASURE IT.

LOVE IS ONLY FELT IN THE HEART.

♡ ♡ ♡ ♡ ♡ ♡ ♡ ♡ ♡ ♡ ♡ ♡ ♡ ♡ ♡ ♡ ♡ ♡

It is easy to see with the example of love that some of our most important and treasured experiences in life are not felt with hands or seen with eyes, but they are as real as anything else that we can see and feel.

Through the mission and ministry of the Holy Ghost, we can learn the truthfulness of things in a similar way—by feeling them. I am writing this chapter on a fast Sunday. Today in our ward we had person after person stand up and bear testimony of the gospel. Except for the kid who breathed into the microphone for ten seconds before his dad came running up to get him off the stand, or the crazy lady who thought it was just open mic night, almost everyone else started several phrases with, "I know . . ." "I know God lives." "I know Jesus is my Savior." "I know the Church is God's Church." After every testimony line they gave, I wanted to ask a follow-up question from the back of the room, "But how do you know??" What if I asked you that about something you believe? If you said, "I KNOW GOD LIVES," and I said, "How do you know?," what would you say? WHAT IS YOUR EVIDENCE OF THAT?

I love the answer that one of my favorite prophets from the Book of Mormon gave to that question. The prophet is Alma—I just love that guy. Do you remember his story? This is the Alma who was famous for living a thug life even though his dad was the prophet. He was a naughty kid, and it took an angel coming and spiritually karate chopping him off his punk train to get him to wake up. But literally the angel knocked him out. TKO. For three days he was in a dream-like coma and felt the pains of a damned soul until his heart turned and was set on the rescue of Jesus. He did the most miraculous spiritual 180 and became a more powerful witness for Christ than he had been an agent of bad. Wild story. But such a good one!

During one of his visits to a branch of the Church, Alma stood up—maybe in testimony meeting—and gave a memorable and heart-thumping testimony of Jesus and the miracle of conversion. Toward the end of it, he asked, "Do ye not suppose that I know of these things myself? Behold, I testify unto you that I do know that these things whereof I have spoken are true." And then maybe someone in the back asked how he knew, because he went straight to it and said, "And how do ye suppose that I know of their surety?" Are you ready for this answer?

> ## "BEHOLD, I SAY UNTO YOU THEY ARE MADE KNOWN UNTO ME BY THE HOLY SPIRIT OF GOD.
>
> Behold I have FASTED and PRAYED many days that I might know these things of myself. And now I do know of myself that they are true; for the Lord God hath made them manifest unto me BY HIS HOLY SPIRIT" (Alma 5:45–46).

Say what? The Holy Spirit? That sounds like it would be the right answer if you came and visited my ward. But Alma? That's how he knows? After all he has experienced? What about the angel that drop-kicked you on the road? Don't you think that was more memorable? Don't you think that would wake up the fourteen-year-olds in the room? "How do you know, Alma?" they ask all skeptical-like. "Oh, you know. I. Saw. An. Angel. I saw father Lehi sitting on a throne. I was in a coma and Jesus rescued me." Those seem like much more convincing arguments. But nope. Of all he could've said,

ALMA TOLD THEM THAT THE EXPERIENCE MOST **MEANINGFUL** TO HIM WAS A VISIT TO HIS HEART FROM THE **HOLY SPIRIT TESTIFYING** OF TRUTH.

President Joseph Fielding Smith once taught another "tough-to-believe" truth along the same lines. He said, "The Lord has taught that there is a stronger witness than seeing a personage, even of seeing the Son of God in a vision.

"Impressions on the soul that come from the Holy Ghost are far more significant than a vision.

"When Spirit speaks to spirit, the imprint upon the soul is far more difficult to erase. Every member of the church should have impressions that Jesus is the Son of God indelibly pictured on his soul through the witness of the Holy Ghost."[14]

Wow, right? The ability of the Holy Ghost to witness truth to us is so powerful that its impact would be more meaningful than seeing a personal vision—EVEN A VISION OF JESUS.

There might be some reading this who don't believe that or think, *yeah, that's not me*. Listen—I get it. It's hard to believe. That's because seeing a vision would have a wow factor to it. Like a firework. But just like a firework, it would fade. Somehow the Holy Ghost has the ability to connect on a spirit-to-spirit level and light a fire *in* us. That flame starts small. It may not be as impressive as a firework at first, but what starts out as a small flicker can over time become a bonfire of belief. SO WHAT IF WE STILL FEEL THE FLAMES ARE SMALL? Can we really say we know something is true at that point? Can we stand confidently in testimony meeting and use that very phrase, "I know," if all we have are sparks in our soul?

If Alma were in the room, I think he might say something similar to us that he said to the questioning people in Alma 32. When they were looking for a witness—for a chance to say, "I know"—Alma suggested to them an experiment. Yep, you read that right. A spiritual experiment. Crossing worlds here. In the experiment, he asked the Saints to compare a truth to a seed and to make a place in their heart to plant that truth in there. Planting it would mean to choose to believe it—without much evidence. He then said, "If ye do not cast it out by unbelief, that ye will resist the Spirit of the Lord, behold, it will begin to swell within your breasts; and when you feel these swelling motions, ye will begin to say within yourselves—IT MUST NEEDS BE THAT THIS IS A GOOD SEED, . . . for it beginneth to enlarge my soul; yea, it beginneth to enlighten my understanding, yea, it beginneth to be delicious to me" (Alma 32:28).

Did you catch what Alma said would happen if the seed was good? It would *begin* to swell in your heart, and *begin* to enlarge your soul—or lead you to love more and want to do good more. He said it would *begin* to enlighten your mind—or give you the feeling like the light is starting to come on. And it would *begin* to be delicious to you—I love that one! The truth would just taste good. These feelings—feelings that come from the Holy Ghost—are your evidence that the truth is good.

Maybe you can't say you **know** with one-hundred-percent certainty **it is true** yet, but you can start by saying **it is good.**

Did you catch the repeated word? BEGIN. All of those would BEGIN to happen. And even though it is only a BEGINNING, it is still happening, and you could honestly stand and say, "I *know* it is good. And I CAN SENSE THE START OF CHANGES IN ME because of it." That is a beautiful beginning, and Alma said if you continue to nourish that knowledge (or continue to choose to believe it enough to live by it), eventually it will grow bigger and bigger and your faith and testimony in it will become more and more sure until "it shall take root; and behold it shall be a tree springing up unto everlasting life" (Alma 32:41). Your experiences yesterday with these good feelings give you the courage to continue to trust today. And the experiences you have today will fuel your courage to keep believing tomorrow. Each day, you are adding a STICK TO THE FIRE. And every now and then you might even get to see a FIREWORK. The more experiences people have with the Holy Ghost, the more confident they become in saying, "I know." But remember that THIS IS A JOURNEY. A journey you take *with* the Holy Ghost. We keep believing, and nourishing, and experiencing, and He patiently and consistently witnesses to us again and again and our confidence grows stronger by the day.

HE IS PATIENT AND KIND AND KNOWS **THIS WILL TAKE TIME.** HE IS IN IT FOR THE LONG HAUL.

As a missionary, it was my job to help people realize what this journey looked like and what it meant to learn something was true. In our mission, we called people learning about the gospel "investigators." I didn't love the word because it had a funky Sherlock Holmes vibe. But they really were solving a mystery. The mystery was whether the words of this nineteen-year-old kid from America speaking broken Korean could actually be true. You see, when you first hear the gospel, your initial reaction is,

> "THAT'S TOO GOOD TO BE TRUE!"

As a missionary I would say back, "I know. I know. It is a wild truth to believe, but you don't have to take my word for it. You can discover truth on your own." Then I would share some verses from the Book of Mormon that missionaries all over the world love to share. The verses come from Moroni. They start with Moroni challenging readers of the book to think about the goodness of God—particularly how good He has been to them. Then he asks them to read the book and let the messages in it sink in (Alma might call this planting a seed ☺). Then he says this: "I would exhort you that ye would ASK GOD . . . if these things are not true; and if ye shall ask WiTH A SiNCERE HEART, with REAL iNTENT, having FAiTH iN CHRiST, he will manifest the truth of it unto you, by the power of the Holy Ghost. And by the power of the Holy Ghost ye may know the truth of all things" (Moroni 10:4–5). We have already talked about what that might be like for Him to "manifest the truth." But how do I know if I know? What is cool is Moroni actually answers that in the next verse. A lot of missionaries don't go on to the next verse—and it might be my favorite. Moroni then says, "And whatsoever thing is good is just and true" (Moroni 10:6). There it is again.

IF IT IS GOOD, THEN IT IS TRUE. If it brings peace, or enlarges your heart, or enlightens your mind, you can say that you *know* it is good. And remember, if IT IS GOOD, THEN IT IS FROM GOD.

This is an experiment that all of us take in our lives. Everyone who says they "know" started this same way and then had the Holy Ghost witness to them it was true. Some of my own beginnings actually started on that RV trip across America. I walked into the Sacred Grove as a fourteen-year-old boy with a challenge from my grandma—my personal Moroni—to sneak away from the group for a minute and find a quiet place to pray. Sneaking seemed more fun than praying at that point in my life, but I remember being drawn to

the idea in a way that surprised and intrigued me. I did both, and something happened inside my heart that morning.

> (A LITTLE FLAME WAS LIT THERE IN THOSE WOODS THAT HAS GROWN UP INTO SOMETHING MORE.)

I walked out knowing that something good happened there. Something I am still experiencing and feeling. But I could stand today and tell you that I know God Almighty lives and speaks to His children. I know Jesus Christ is the tender Redeemer of the world. The light, the truth, and the way. And I know that Joseph Smith was called by Them and visited by Them in that sacred spot of trees I went to over twenty years ago. THOSE ARE TRUTHS THAT BEGAN THERE WHEN THE HOLY GHOST FIRST TURNED MY HEART TO THEM. When He first made me feel they were good. When He first shined a light on those truths and made them sparkle. And it left a fingerprint on my heart.

For the Day You Wish You Were Better ...

THE SANCTIFIER

Every year at Christmas, all of my kids put ridiculous things on their Christmas lists. I don't blame them. It's their only shot at something good all year. And I'm a believer in dreaming big—so write whatever you want, I say! Hoping is good for the soul. And so is hearing no. This year, they all thought they wanted a cell phone—even the ones who can't read. That is debated fiercely in the parents' world—when kids are ready for a cell phone. CAN THEY HANDLE THE RESPONSIBILITY AND THE RISKS? Will they go way over on the data charges? All the things!

This debate happens with everything. How long until the little boys can watch *Jurassic Park* without getting nightmares? And what about curfews? When are they ready to leave home with friends and be trusted that they will not end up in jail? Or when can they be left at home to babysit without burning down the neighborhood? And I'm so glad the government decided when they can drive. My

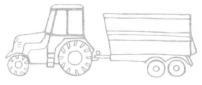

farmer friends were all driving tractors at five years old, but there is not a prayer that some of my kids will get behind a wheel before they are twenty-five. You're welcome. The same question of when someone is ready could be asked about making covenants at baptism. There is no way our little boy will find a cell phone under the Christmas tree, but God thinks he is ready for eternal covenants through baptism.

SOME PEOPLE ASK THE QUESTION ABOUT KIDS BEING BAPTIZED AT AGE EIGHT, "DO THEY EVEN KNOW WHAT THEY ARE DOING?" I can still remember the temperature of the water of the baptismal font when I stepped into it—a little on the cold side. I remember my friend Brent dropping his piece of cake into his younger brother's drink at the after party. I remember the restaurant we went to eat out at that night and even where I sat at the table. I also remember the next day opening up my new brown leather journal that my grandparents had given me, sitting at the kitchen table, and writing this line:

" I promise for the rest of my life to never sin. Shouldn't be that hard. "

I distinctly remember thinking that and writing it. I remember people talking at my baptism about how I would make mistakes and sin the rest of my life, but I could always be forgiven. I rolled my eyes as I wrote in my journal. I actually mumbled under my breath, "Bring it on." I legit did not think it was going to be hard at all—in fact, I was a little bored of thinking about living life because of how easy it was going to be. Piece of cake (not the one Brent dropped in the drink).

But, as you might guess, I dropped the ball on that easy goal of mine. That very day, in fact. I yelled at my younger sister. I was heartbroken. I couldn't believe it. My streak hadn't even lasted a day. It shocked me. How could I have done that? The same day!! I NEEDED A DO-OVER. I wanted so desperately to be baptized again. It was a moment of weakness. Now I knew. I could do it this time if I could just be baptized once more.

That wasn't the only time in my life when I thought that way.

I remember another day sitting in Sunday School and hearing the story of an eighty-two-year-old grandma who had gotten baptized in our stake. Lucky! She lived her whole life, and then at eighty-two got all of her sins washed away. Now she is golden. What eighty-two-year-old even sins? I remember wishing again—IF ONLY I COULD GET REBAPTIZED.

The ordinance of baptism is wonderful because it provides an initial cleansing. We use phrases like "wash away my sins" that are obviously in reference to the water in the baptismal font.

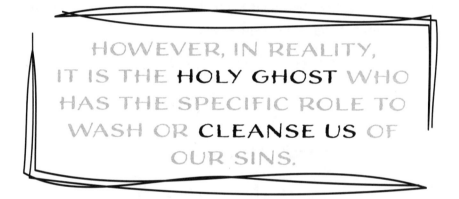

HOWEVER, IN REALITY, IT IS THE **HOLY GHOST** WHO HAS THE SPECIFIC ROLE TO WASH OR **CLEANSE US** OF OUR SINS.

Elder David A. Bednar once taught, "THE HOLY GHOST IS A SANCTIFIER WHO CLEANSES AND BURNS DROSS AND EVIL OUT OF HUMAN SOULS AS THOUGH BY FIRE." Because the power is not in the water, but in the Spirit, this can happen again and again. One of the times we focus on it is during the sacrament. Elder Bednar also said, "The ordinance of the sacrament is a holy and repeated invitation to repent sincerely and to be renewed spiritually. . . . As we prepare conscientiously and participate in this holy ordinance with a broken heart and a contrite spirit, then the promise is that we may *always* have the Spirit of the Lord to be with us. And by the sanctifying power of the Holy Ghost as our constant companion, we can *always* retain a remission of our sins."[15] Yo! That is a word! Essentially,

THE **SACRAMENT** CAN BECOME ANOTHER **BAPTISM** EXPERIENCE FOR US EACH WEEK.

I wish I would've known that the day after my baptism and on the day I sat in Sunday School jealous of the eighty-two-year-old grandma. In reality, she would say that I was actually the lucky one. This is what I've learned since then.

IT IS THROUGH THE MERITS, ← → MERCY, AND GRACE ← OF JESUS CHRIST THAT WE ARE FORGIVEN AND CLEANSED OF OUR SINS.

It is NOT THE WATER and it is NOT THE SACRAMENT. Through those ordinances, we invite the Holy Ghost into our lives. It's the way we choose to have Him come. It's the way we exercise our free will to receive that gift of cleansing. IT IS THE HOLY GHOST THAT DELIVERS THAT CLEANSING AND SANCTIFYING POWER OF JESUS INTO OUR HEARTS.

He waits for that invitation. This is how Elder D. Todd Christofferson described it: "The gift of the Holy Ghost . . . is the MESSENGER OF GRACE by which the blood of Christ is applied to take away our sins and sanctify us (see 2 Nephi 31:17). It is the gift by which Adam was 'quickened in the inner man' (Moses 6:65)."[16]

In the scriptures, there is a difference between being cleansed of our sins and being sanctified. You may remember that word *sanctify* from the sacrament prayers. We ask God to "bless and sanctify" the bread and water. To SANCTIFY MEANS TO MAKE HOLY—specifically to become holy for a certain purpose—God's purpose. THE SPIRIT NOT ONLY CLEANSES US, BUT HE WORKS ON US TO MAKE US HOLY. We didn't come to earth to become cleansed. We came here already clean. Do you know any sinner babies? If we went back to heaven clean, we would be going back the way we came. We are trying to live in a way to become God's holy people. To be changed into someone better. Someone more like Him. This process is also known in scriptures as "becoming a new creature" (1 Corinthians 5:17), becoming "a saint" (Mosiah 3:19), or being born again. This is the work of the Spirit in us—to turn us into a new creature and Saint.

Because of the gift of the Holy Ghost, we can have His essential help on our journeys "to become" during our entire lives. The sooner that begins, the more time the Holy Ghost has to work in us in a more consistent way.

That is why the eighty-two-year-old grandma would call me the lucky one.

One night, when Jesus was alone, a man named Nicodemus came to see Him. Nicodemus had heard of Jesus's miracles and was beginning to be convinced that He was more than just a normal preacher of the scriptures. Perhaps sensing that Nicodemus was wondering what to do next in his life, Jesus taught him, "Except a man be born again, he cannot see the kingdom of God." Nicodemus was a little confused, so he then asked one of the dumbest questions recorded in the scriptures. "How can a man be born when he is old? can he enter the second time into his mother's womb, and be born?" Oh, dear. Bless his heart. Jesus then clarified, "Except a man be born of water and of the Spirit, he cannot enter into the kingdom of God" (John 3:3–5).

Being born of **water** is **baptism.**
Being born of the **Spirit** is **conversion** or **sanctification** (being made holy).

Have you ever noticed that one of the symbols of baptism is a representation of birth? When you go down into the water, you are symbolically like a little baby who is immersed and then comes out of the water like a baby does out of the water-filled womb of a mom. A NEW LIFE!

I have been present for six births in my life. One of them, the most exciting of them, happened in our bathroom because Jenny has the pain tolerance of a pioneer and we couldn't make it to the hospital in time. Remind me to tell you all the fun parts of that story another day. But just remember I am now officially a doctor since I delivered a baby at my house. If any women are reading this (particularly the woman I am married to), they are going to disagree with what I just said. "No," they may say in a bothered voice, "*you* absolutely did not deliver a baby. *I* did." And that would be true. I actually just caught a baby. Interestingly, at the births of all of our babies, no one congratulated me for a job well done. That's because I didn't do anything except refill the ice cup. More importantly, no one congratulates the baby, either. Because the baby did even less. WHEN A BABY IS BORN, IT IS THE MOTHER WHO DOES ALL OF THE HARD LABOR. It is through her struggle, blood, sweat, tears, and visit to death's door that a baby comes into the world. (Everyone go thank your mom!) The same is true of our spiritual rebirth.

We make ourselves **available** and **choose** to be reborn, but it is **through Jesus's** labor, blood, sweat, tears, and visit through death's door that we are actually able to be reborn.

The Spirit is who brings all of the power of His sacrifice into our souls.

The Lord told Adam, "As ye were born into the world by water, and blood, and the spirit, . . . even so ye must be born again into the kingdom of heaven, of water, and of the Spirit, and be cleansed by blood, even the blood of mine Only Begotten; that ye might be sanctified from all sin" (Moses 6:59). When a baby is born, there is a lot of water, blood, and spirit. In that same way, when we are born again, we are born again through water (baptism), blood (the Savior's Atonement), and the Spirit (the messenger of that grace).

THE BAPTISM OF THE SPIRIT IS THE CONTINUAL INFLUENCE OF THE SANCTIFYING AND CLEANSING POWER OF THE HOLY GHOST THROUGHOUT OUR LIVES.

We try hard to be immersed in His presence. Baptism by water takes about ten seconds (and thank goodness, because I cannot hold my breath for very long). THE BAPTISM OF THE SPIRIT IS A PROCESS THAT TAKES AN ENTIRE LIFETIME.

What does that process look like? There is an old legend that you may be familiar with. It is the story of a boy whose wise grandfather chief teaches him that inside every human soul are two wolves fighting viciously for the ownership of the soul. When the little boy asks his grandfather which wolf wins, the grandfather replies, "The one you feed." This idea is all over the world. WE ALL SENSE iT—A BATTLE BETWEEN GOOD AND EViL iN OUR SOULS. Some people describe it with the wolf story and others tell it in cartoons with an angel on one shoulder and the devil on the other (like Kronk!).

King Benjamin used these words to describe the same story: "For the natural man [wolf number one or shoulder devil] is an enemy to God, and has been from the fall of Adam, and will be, forever and ever, UNLESS HE YiELDS TO THE ENTiCiNGS OF THE HOLY SPiRiT (wolf number two or shoulder angel), and putteth off the natural man and becometh a saint through the atonement of Christ the Lord" (Mosiah 3:19).

Each day, as we live our lives, we are tempted by the devil and enticed by the Holy Spirit to choose one way or the other. As we yield or give in to the Holy Spirit, we exercise our agency and allow the Holy Spirit to bring the cleansing, sanctifying, and changing power of Jesus into our hearts and character. Usually this change is happening without us even knowing it.

It is a **slow process,** and God has all the time in the world, so **be patient** with yourself! He is being patient with you.

Elder David B. Haight was a member of the Quorum of the Twelve Apostles when I was younger. I once heard him tell a story about seeing this change happening in his wife. When they were a younger couple, they were called to serve as mission president and companion for the Scotland Mission. This was before planes were popular for flying across the ocean, so he and his wife took a cruise ship to get across the sea to their mission. Not bad! The cruise ship had a movie theater on it, so on the way over, they watched the movie that was playing.

After three years serving in Scotland, they hopped back on another cruise ship to sail back home. It just so happened that the same movie was playing on the way home as the way there. (I guess they didn't make as many movies back then—thank goodness for the abundance of movies *and* planes in our day!) Sister Haight remembered seeing the movie and how much she had loved it, so she decided to watch it again on the way home. Elder Haight said that when they walked out of the movie, she turned to him and said, "Oh, that's too bad. Why did they go and ruin such a perfectly good movie by adding all that bad stuff into it? They shouldn't have changed it." At first he didn't know what she was talking about, but then he realized something powerful. THE MOVIE DIDN'T CHANGE—SHE DID. For three years she fed the right wolf, and she was more of a Saint on the way home than she had been on the way there.

{ THE HOLY GHOST HAD BEEN INVITED AND THEN SLOWLY BUT SURELY SANCTIFIED HER SOUL. }

As you look back over your life, you will be able to see the changes that are slowly happening in you. Are there movies or jokes you used to like a year ago that don't appeal to you much anymore? Are you kinder to people than you were in the past? Alma asked a group of friends, "Have ye spiritually been born of God? Have ye received his image in your countenances? HAVE YE EXPERIENCED THIS MIGHTY CHANGE IN YOUR HEARTS? . . . If ye have experienced a change of heart, and if ye have felt to sing the song of redeeming love, I would ask, can ye feel so now?" (Alma 5:14, 26).

I love those questions. They are so good to ask.

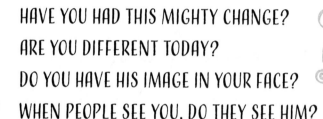

HAVE YOU HAD THIS MIGHTY CHANGE?
ARE YOU DIFFERENT TODAY?
DO YOU HAVE HIS IMAGE IN YOUR FACE?
WHEN PEOPLE SEE YOU, DO THEY SEE HIM?

Can you sing that song of praise—the one you want to bust out when you feel forgiven of sins? The one with the second verse about how you are so different today than you were back then?

I will be the first one to say that when I ask myself these questions, I realize that I am not quite yet who I want to be (and that was putting it nicely). It will definitely be a long, slow, but mighty change. I am so glad I have had the opportunity since I was eight to experience this more consistently in my life. But no matter how long it takes me (and I am near the back of the line—not even kidding!), I will also be the first to say that even with someone like me it is possible. It is POSSIBLE first and foremost BECAUSE OF JESUS. And it is possible BECAUSE OF THE GIFT OF THE HOLY GHOST. They work together tirelessly to bring about this miracle in us. Every day—one day at a time.

And this is true for all of us. One night, the wonderful and admirable prophet Isaiah had a dream where he walked into the temple. You can read this in Isaiah 6. When he got inside, he saw the Lord sitting upon a throne, surrounded by angels of fire. Immediately, he bowed his head and let out a groan, "Woe is me! for I am undone; because I am a man of unclean lips, and I dwell in the midst of a people of unclean lips."

He did not feel comfortable standing in the holy **presence of God.** He was sinful and lived among sinful people. What if he contaminated that holy place?!

But then one of those angels grabbed some tongs and picked up a red-hot coal from the burning altar and laid it on his mouth and said, "Thine iniquity is taken away, and thy sin purged." In the ancient temple, the altar with the burning sacrifice was a symbol of the Atonement of Jesus Christ. In his dream, Isaiah was seeing a symbolic vision of what happens in our lives. I like to think of that angel as a symbolic representative of the Holy Ghost. The one who brings the red-hot love and power of Jesus's Atonement to us—to cleanse us and sanctify us. After this happens, the Lord then asks, "Whom shall I send, and who will go for us?" Isaiah immediately calls out, "Here am I; send me" (Isaiah 6:5, 7–8).

Isaiah does not contaminate the holy place with his sins and imperfections, but instead, **The Holy Spirit burns them out** and contaminates Isaiah with <u>His</u> goodness—the goodness of Jesus.

I think about this story occasionally when I press the bread and water cup against my lips during the sacrament. Emblems that are brought to me from an altar by a messenger.

In those moments, I relate to Isaiah, who walked into the holy place with his head bowed—ashamed of who he was—feeling unfit to be in the presence of God or beating himself up for not being good enough yet. Like that boy on the day after his baptism, wishing he could be someone different. And then *afterward*, after the Holy Spirit delivers and confirms the cleansing, sanctifying, changing love of Christ, and POURS SOME CONFIDENCE INTO HIS HEART, and pulls him close in a holy embrace to whisper in his ear a reminder that the journey is still continuing, that HE IS NOT A DISAPPOINTMENT, and that He will be right there next to him until the very end—after all of that—that same Isaiah lifts his head boldly before the throne of grace and calls out to the Lord to send him wherever He needs him. Isaiah feels like he was made holy for a certain purpose. He was underqualified and too young and maybe not ready on his own.

But with the help of the Father, the Son, and the Holy Spirit, he felt **on fire** with confidence to continue the journey.

Interestingly, he even used the same words Jesus used when the Father first asked in the premortal world whom He should send. "Here am I; send me." Isaiah was receiving Jesus's image in his countenance. And I bet he felt like singing the song of redeeming love.

THE GUIDE

One year for my birthday, my mom and dad gave me scuba certification classes. It was perfect, because Jenny and I had just made our plans to move to Hawaii and I was stoked to both learn to scuba dive and then get a chance to live as part merman while going to school out there. It was as dreamy as I thought it was going to be, by the way. Not the classes—they were so boring—but scuba diving off the Hawaiian islands was a win! Except this one time. My mom and sister Jacquelyn had come out to visit us, and we all decided we would go on a drift dive together. A DRIFT DIVE is when the BOAT DROPS YOU OFF IN A CERTAIN SPOT where there is a strong underwater current AND THEN PICKS YOU UP IN AN ENTIRELY DIFFERENT ONE—usually pretty far away from the drop-off spot. The guide you go with knows the underwater currents really well and has a GPS to be able to match up and find the boat once everyone starts running low on air. We all dropped into the water and started to lower down to the ocean floor. When you scuba dive, you have to go down slowly, and every few feet, you plug your nose and blow out to put pressure in your ears so they equalize with the pressure of the water and don't hurt when you go deeper. My mom, who had broken her nose dancing several years before, had a hard time getting her ears to equalize with the pressure. The guide had miscounted the number in our group, so by the time my mom finally got to the bottom, the group had left us and already swum away—nowhere to be

found. She and Jacquelyn both looked at me underwater and started pointing a few different directions and then put up their arms as if they were asking, "Which way did they go?" I put my hands up like the shrugging "I don't know" emoji and then pointed up so we could use words instead of trying to guess underwater sign language. We all bobbed on top of the water for a minute looking around. The waves on the surface were coming across in large swells, but every few seconds they would flatten out just enough that you could look around and see if there was any sign of the boat. And there wasn't. ALL WE COULD SEE WERE MILES OF OCEAN. Out in the far distance we could see the mountains on land, but we had gone way out of the bay and beyond the reef. That's when I started to panic a little. THE BOAT HAD LEFT US, AND SO HAD THE GUIDE.

I told my mom and sister to go down and swim below and I would swim on the surface. That way I could always make sure we were at least heading toward land, and if the boat ever did come back it might see where we were. Staying put in a moving ocean was not exactly an option. It didn't take very long before the currents on the surface and the currents beneath the water were pulling us away from each other. THEY COULDN'T SEE ME, I COULDN'T SEE LAND, AND THERE WAS NO WAY OF SIGNALING THE BOAT. To make matters worse, I had just watched a shark attack movie the week before. Not my best move. But the worst move of the day definitely belonged to the scuba guide for leaving behind three amateur scuba-ers to navigate the world's oceans on their own. In case it isn't obvious, we survived! The boat eventually found us before the sharks, and I am pretty sure we got a refund.

I can't help but think of that story when I hear this quote from Elder Joseph B. Wirthlin:

"The gift of **the Holy Ghost** may be likened to a sure, **personal compass** to provide lifesaving vision, wisdom, and insight as a spiritual window. The Holy Ghost gives us clear **guidance and direction** in a world of unanchored faith." [17]

That is what we needed out there. A personal compass, some wisdom, and some lifesaving something. That is an amazing promise. SOMETIMES LIFE FEELS LIKE THAT HOUR WE SPENT ALONE OUT IN THE MIDDLE OF THE SEA—bobbing around, not really knowing where to go or what to choose. I have never felt more helpless in my life. What was I supposed to do?? One choice could lead us to the boat and another one could lead us to finding Jonah at the bottom of a whale. All of the decisions and the unknowns of life can be overwhelming. FOR MOMENTS LIKE THAT, WE HAVE BEEN PROMISED A GUIDE— one that *wouldn't* abandon us, but would give us wisdom and show us the way. I should point out right here that for a while, we did float out in the sea feeling like we were abandoned. It is interesting that with all the places we could've floated to, the boat knew how to find us. Maybe we weren't in as much trouble as we thought we were.

Maybe we weren't really abandoned, but we only felt abandoned. We are going to talk about this a little bit more in another chapter— about what to do in those moments you feel abandoned—but perhaps my best bit of advice I can give right now is one I learned from a movie—to just keep swimming. KEEP GOING. THE LIFEBOAT IS NOT FAR. And if it comes to it, the Lord knows how to help us walk on water.

He might let you swim, but He will not let you drown.

You and I have had to and will have to make so many decisions throughout our lives. Some of them don't matter too much, like black or pinto beans, and some of them may feel like the whole world is depending on them. What school do I go to? Which job should I choose? What am I supposed to do about so-and-so? How do I deal with my dad? We make decisions about school, relationships, work, ways to spend time and money, what to do about certain situations with friends, and on and on and on.

THE GOOD NEWS IS THAT WE NEVER HAVE TO MAKE A DECISION **ON OUR OWN.** WE DO NOT HAVE TO NAVIGATE THIS LIFE BY OURSELVES. WE HAVE THE SPIRIT, WHO IS BOTH **ALL-KNOWING AND ALL-LOVING.**

That combination makes Him the perfect person to deliver advice and guidance to us on behalf of the Father when we are trying to make a choice at all of the forks in the road that come during life.

Elder Richard G. Scott was once reminiscing about his life before he was a full-time Apostle. He said, "[In my work] it just seemed natural to turn to the Lord to ask for guidance. I've never separated church, professional life, family life, or personal life into little compartments; I'VE JUST FELT THAT THE SPIRIT CAN GUIDE IN ALL OF THOSE. . . . [He is] absolutely aware and very interested in giving us support in whatever we do in life, our professional life included."[18] That list includes everything that you are doing and are passionate about in life. His point is that the Spirit cares about all those things. Nephi doubled down on Elder Scott's promise and said,

> "IF YE WILL ENTER IN BY THE
> WAY, AND RECEIVE THE HOLY
> GHOST, IT WILL SHOW UNTO YOU
> ALL THINGS WHAT YE SHOULD
> DO" (2 NEPHI 32:5).

 ALL THINGS!

He not only cares, but He wants to be involved in helping us navigate it all.

Several years ago, I came to a fork in the road with my job. I had worked at the same one for several years and had started to get bored with it, so I was looking for a change. In a conversation with a good friend of mine, I told him I was on the hunt, and as luck would have it, he already had something waiting for me. It seemed perfect. The new job was exciting, and I would get to spend time with one of my favorite friends, make more money, and work with super cool people with a way more flexible schedule and chill vibe and atmosphere (no church clothes and not as many meetings! Bless!!). And the benefits of it could include basketball tickets, Christmas bonuses, motorcycles, and really fun opportunities. My other job used to give us a book for a Christmas bonus—but they stopped doing that and switched to a Christmas card. So, yeah. . . . But despite the lame things about my job at the time, I actually loved it. So I thought about it a lot, prayed about it, weighed all the possibilities, decided that I wanted the new job, and finally moved forward with my choice. I was going to switch. I was pumped about it. I told my family my decision at dinner, told my bosses at work the change that was coming, and started down a path full speed ahead. The day before the decision would have been practically irreversible, I did not sleep a single wink. I must have counted 20,000 sheep. I HAD THE MOST INTENSE PRESSING ON MY MIND AND HEART THAT WHAT I WAS ABOUT TO DO WAS THE WRONG DECISION. I could not believe it. I thought it had been an inspired decision. I had prayed about it and felt good to move forward. I had already told everyone what I was doing. Going back on this decision would be so awkward. The conversations I would need to have would possibly burn bridges and make me look irresponsible and irrational. Despite all of that, I knew what I needed to do. This was hard, but it was the right decision.

Today I still look back and wonder what would have happened if I had chosen that other job. I don't see any danger in it, and I see a lot of potential in that first choice to change. There is no obvious reason I shouldn't have done it, and sometimes I still question and wonder why the Spirit didn't tell me earlier (maybe He did!). Because to be honest, the decision process was really difficult. I didn't hear a voice from heaven tell me to switch jobs. It just felt like it was okay. BUT THE FEELINGS TO BACK OUT OF IT WERE STRONGER. It wasn't fear—I had been through that. It was firm but also encouraging about the future. I felt like there were opportunities ahead that I needed to stick around for.

I AM STILL TRYING TO LISTEN TO AND BE GUIDED BY THE SPIRIT. IT IS SOMETHING I AM LEARNING HOW TO DO.

But when I thought about the new job, I felt uncomfortable about it. When I thought about my old one, I felt encouraged and confident. I took these feelings as impressions. After all the awkward reversals, I STILL FELT GOOD ABOUT MY CHOICE. That felt like another confirmation to me. And even though I was really disappointed, I was also thankful that the Spirit was helping me make the turns that would lead me to the happiest places. I trust Him in that. And it took trust, because the process was sort of messy.

For people like me,

this promise of guidance is one of the most golden.

I have the absolute worst sense of direction and am terrible at making decisions. It is bad, y'all. We lived in our old house for ten years, and I would still ask Jenny every week which way to turn out of our driveway to get to church. The day I got my license at age sixteen, my parents sent me to the store to buy something and I had no idea how to get home. Once, for work, I delivered a wedding cake to a hotel in downtown Houston and got lost somewhere. It must have been a bad part of town, because the lady from work who came with me to deliver the cake was crying and praying the whole time in the back seat. I cannot live without the maps app on my phone. It saves me every day. God bless you, Google!

That same Nephi who gave the promise about the Lord showing us all things woke up one morning and found his own GPS gift from the Lord—the Liahona, a metal ball sitting on the front porch of the family tent. (This was before there was ever Amazon Prime, so a legit miracle!) As you may remember, THE LIAHONA HAD SPINDLES THAT POINTED IN THE DIRECTION THE LORD WANTED THEM TO GO. It was a compass! From time to time, words would even show up on it giving them specific instructions. When I read about their family being led by the Liahona, I am certain that Google and Apple stole the idea for Google Maps and iMessage from the story. And second, I believe that THIS STORY IS GOD TEACHING them and us through AN OBJECT LESSON ABOUT the marvelous gift of guidance from the HOLY GHOST.

In that story of the Liahona, we learn that when they followed the directions on the ball, it not only eventually led them to the promised land, but along the way it "led [them] in the more fertile parts of the wilderness" (1 Nephi 16:16). There are, scattered throughout the Arabian Peninsula (the spot Lehi and his family were traveling), pockets that you would think were a tropical island. Most of the area is hot, sandy, and lifeless, but there are oases scattered, little mini Hawaiis, and riverbeds of life to follow if you know where to go.

> The Holy Ghost has the eventual goal and purpose of leading us to the promised land—to eternal life in the presence of the Father and the Son. He also wants to lead us through pieces of paradise along the way.

There are several ways to get from A to Z—the Spirit wants to guide us and lead us on the best possible route.

This does not mean that we will not experience hardship and disappointment and tragedy in our lives. Keep in mind that most of the time Nephi's family was traveling it was through barren desert, living on raw meat, with brothers who wanted to kill their dad. They were definitely in a desert place—but they were also definitely being led by the Lord. Getting us to eternal life is more important to the Lord than comfort or a certain school, job, or spouse.

WE HAVE TO REMEMBER THAT BEING LED BY THE HOLY GHOST DOESN'T MEAN THAT LIFE IS GOING TO BE EASY OR CAREFREE.

That is not the promise. We are all learning to listen, and having the courage to follow (especially if it is different than what we hoped) is all a part of the journey as well.

Yes, He will lead us to fertile places, but no, those won't be the only places we travel.

Another prophet from the Book of Mormon who was on his own journey taught us what it might look like to be led by the Holy Ghost. The brother of Jared (whose story you can read about in Ether 2–3) was also going with his family to a promised land when they got to a spot in their journey where they didn't know what to do. After arriving at a beautiful beach, the family was instructed by the Lord to build barges they could cross the ocean in. (I wonder if they really wanted to just stay at that beach!) When they were  done building them, the brother of Jared noticed three problems—they had no light, no air, and no way of steering. These probably won't be the same problems that you have, but you can do the same thing the brother of Jared did, and ask the Lord—*what next?* The answers the brother of Jared got teach us different ways that the Spirit might guide us in our lives.

For the problem with air, THE SPIRIT JUST TAUGHT HIM EXACTLY WHAT HE SHOULD DO—cut some holes in the top and bottom that you can plug up when your barge goes underwater and open when it surfaces. Easy. Sometimes this happens—we will get a thought or idea that pops into our minds that just makes sense. The solution. Or maybe the advice will come through someone else and we will know that person was speaking with inspiration because it will just feel right. Sometimes it is as simple as following the arrows on the Liahona.

For the light problem, THE SPIRIT ASKED THE BROTHER OF JARED WHAT HE WANTED THE LORD TO DO ABOUT IT. He put the decision-making into the brother of Jared's lap. Sometimes He does this to us, too. He asks us, "What will ye that I should do?" (Ether 2:23). The Lord has given all of us a mind to think, a mouth to speak, hands to do, and feet to move. For a lot of decisions in our lives, the Spirit will encourage us to make our own choice with the promise that He will be with us in whatever we choose. You may remember that the brother of Jared decided to get sixteen small stones and ask the Lord to touch them to make them glow. And He did!! Was that the only solution the brother of Jared could've picked? Probably not. But it was one the brother of Jared thought would work, and the Lord took that decision and made it even better.

For the steering issue, THE SPIRIT SIMPLY PROMISED THE BROTHER OF JARED THAT THE LORD WOULD TAKE CARE OF IT—just get in your barges and let the wind blow you across the sea to the promised land (see Ether 2:25).

If I got to choose how the Spirit guided me, I would pick the first option, ten for ten. I LOVE THE FIRST ONE. Just tell me what to do and I will do it! I hate making decisions. I can't even decide what to order off of a menu. Everyone else can do it so confidently, and I am always asking the waiter to come back to me. That's what makes the second one trickier for me. I have had so many friends and past students come to me looking for advice in their lives. I am so happy to give it, but I also want them to ask for help from heaven. Usually when I say something like that, they tell me that they have been praying about it and have not seemed to get an answer. I always wonder if they are being told "brother of Jared option 2." Perhaps the Spirit is saying to them, "WHY DON'T YOU MAKE THE DECISION?" In those times in my life, I am usually paralyzed with fear. *But what if I choose wrong? What if I ruin future opportunities or chances?* I have learned two truths that have given me courage in those situations.

The **first** is

✳ The Spirit will not let us get very far
in a wrong decision.

If we are heading down a dangerous or wrong path, He will always turn us around in a very clear way. If Siri knows how to reroute us, I promise that God can do it too.

The **second** is

✳ God is bigger than your choices.

Even if you did choose wrong, He could weave that mistake into the pattern of your life and still provide opportunities and blessings and chances for wonderful, amazing things ahead. I promise you that YOU CANNOT RUIN YOUR LIFE or your eternal destiny WHEN YOU ARE TRYING TO TRUST IN THE GOODNESS OF GOD, the forgiveness of Jesus, and the guiding hand of the Holy Spirit. So just make the choice and move ahead—you won't mess up what God has in store for you.

And as far as that third option goes—that one is scarier than the second. These seem to be those times when the Spirit tells you which direction to go but doesn't give you the detailed step-by-step plan for how it will work out. In moments like that, we feel like Nephi, who got no instructions on how to get the brass plates. Nephi said, "I, Nephi, crept into the city and went forth towards the house of Laban. And I was led by the Spirit, not knowing beforehand the things which I should do. Nevertheless I went forth" (1 Nephi 4:5–7).

I LOVE NEPHI'S TRUST IN THE LAST LINE. EVEN THOUGH I DIDN'T KNOW EXACTLY WHAT WOULD HAPPEN, I JUST WENT.

It is thrilling to hear about it in someone else's story—terrifying to have to live it in your own.

It might be helpful for you to hear that I have had a lot more option 2 and 3 experiences in my life than option 1. There have been times when an answer has come so clearly from the Spirit to me. It happens. But most of the time, it is pretty fuzzy and messy for me. There are several spots in the scriptures where we see this pattern. One of my favorites is when Peter, as lead Apostle of the Church, is making a major policy change for the Saints (you can read this in Acts 15). After discussing it with all the other leaders, praying, and having personal experiences, Peter made a decision and explained it by saying (three times): "FOR IT SEEMED GOOD TO THE HOLY GHOST, AND TO US" (Acts 15:28).

I LOVE THAT PHRASE. "IT SEEMED GOOD."

He isn't completely confident, but he is pretty sure he is being led by the Spirit. The Lord lets us struggle through this. We keep learning how to recognize the voice of the Spirit and keep trying to be led by Him. The messiness of it forces us to rely on Him more and more, which is exactly what He wants. It leads to connection and relationship. It leads us to spending more time seeking for, listening to, and wanting the presence and Spirit of God.

IT SEEMS LIKE THE HOLY GHOST IS MORE INTERESTED IN WHO WE BECOME DURING THE JOURNEY.

Let's also not forget that while the brother of Jared and his family were banging around in the barges, perhaps wondering if they had been forgotten, and having no CLUE how long the journey was going to be (Can you even imagine?! It would drive me crazy!!), they would look up into the corner of the barge and see the stone glowing. THERE WERE THE SMALL, CONSTANT REMINDERS ALONG THE WAY THAT GOD WAS STILL IN CHARGE.

When talking about the Liahona, Alma the prophet once told his sons that through "small means it did show unto them marvelous works" (Alma 37:41). Every time I read that, I think to myself—*small!?* I feel like it's a pretty big deal that God made them a magical compass and dropped it on their porch. I don't know if I would call that small. I think what he meant was that

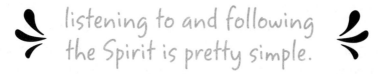

listening to and following
the Spirit is pretty simple.

The whole idea of it. But I also think he believed it's a pretty big deal that God the Third is willing and wanting to guide us through life. And the whole time, as a guide who never leaves us, He gently says, *keep going, keep swimming, keep trusting—I am taking you to land—the promised land.*

For the Day When Things Are Hard . . .

THE COMFORTER

When Jenny was in college, she was the luckiest duck and got to spend a semester studying abroad at the BYU Jerusalem Center—a mini college campus right on the Mount of Olives overlooking the old city of Jerusalem. You would not believe how rad this place is, and you should absolutely Google pictures of it right now. It is on the most prime piece of land in all of Jerusalem. The chapel on campus is slanted with stadium seating so that you are looking down on the microphone podium, which has giant, floor-to-ceiling windows behind it with the most spectacular views. If you are there for a sacrament meeting, you literally look into the area of the Garden of Gethsemane, Calvary's Hill, and the ancient Temple Mount while you take the sacrament. A dream! I am not sure if anyone could listen to the speakers because of how distracting the view would be behind them. Not only is the campus itself beautiful, but the students who study there get to live where Jesus lived, walk where Jesus walked, and swim where Jesus also walked. I drip with jealousy.

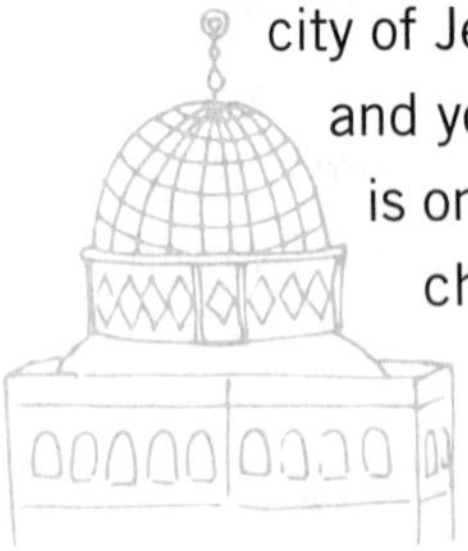

While she was there, EVERY SABBATH MORNING, JENNY WOULD WALK TO THE GARDEN TOMB TO STUDY HER SCRIPTURES (I mean, come on! Who gets that chance??). The Garden Tomb is a flower garden surrounding an open, empty sepulcher that many people believe was the place where Jesus was buried and rose again on the third day. On one particular day, while Jenny was sitting on one of the benches inside the garden area, a commotion erupted just beyond the walls. Soon she could hear yelling, the sound of glass breaking, and the continual gunshots of automatic rifles. The workers scurried to lock the gates and everyone took cover on the inside. A riot had broken out in the streets. While the bullets flew and the chaos swirled on the outside of the walls, Jenny said she was surprised by an inward SENSE of PEACE AND CALM. She was so settled in her heart that she actually just continued to read her scriptures with the sounds and echoes of gunshots in the background. The first time I ever heard that story was in a sacrament meeting talk she was giving. My mouth was open in shock. This kind of stuff only happens in the Mission: Impossible movies—riots and guns and stuff. But what was more surprising was how she described how peaceful she felt during it all. "I NEVER FELT LIKE I WAS iN DANGER. I FELT CALM. PROTECTED." And then she said, "I guess that's kind of like how I feel living in this riotous world too.

> 66 War, chaos, disappointment, and despair swirl around, but because of **what happened in that Garden Tomb** two thousand years ago, the Prince of Peace can still reign and rule inside the walls of my heart. 99

Preach, Jenny! Can we get an amen?

The only reason Jesus's first disciples didn't get shot at back in the day is because guns weren't invented yet. The world has always been under commotion with a hailstorm of something. The night before Jesus's Crucifixion, somewhere near that garden that Jenny had her experience and where Jesus would soon be buried, Jesus promised His disciples, "I will pray the Father, and HE SHALL GiVE you ANOTHER COMFORTER, that he may abide with you for ever; . . . I will not leave you comfortless: I WiLL COME To you" (John 14:16, 18). Knowing the scary future ahead for those eleven disciples and the scary future ahead for *all* disciples, Jesus promised that He would come to us and be with all of us by sending the Comforter.

My favorite part about Jesus's promise is how limitless it is. He said He would abide with us, or stay with us, forever. That means ALWAYS and in ALL CIRCUMSTANCES.

In any situation we would need His COMFORT, HELP, and strength, the Comforter would be there.

And we wouldn't need to go looking for Him—He would come to us.

Do you remember the story of God comforting Elijah in the book of Kings in the Bible? He is the prophet who called down fire from heaven to convince the wicked Queen Jezebel and all of her priests that Jehovah was the one true God (you can read all about it in 1 Kings 18). As spectacular as the miracle was that happened, Jezebel didn't care. She didn't change her ways, and instead she doubled down on her efforts to hunt and kill Elijah the prophet. He had just spent three years in hiding, living in a cave like a bear, and getting his food delivered to him by a raven. And now this! Come on! In his frustration, Elijah went up into the mountains, plopped down under a juniper tree and just went to sleep, wanting to give up (see 1 Kings 19:4). *Okay, Lord, I've had enough. You can take me. I'm not winning this battle. Nothing is going my way. I give up.* What happens next is one of my favorite parts in the Bible. Elijah fell asleep under the tree, and after a little snooze, an angel came and woke him up. "And [Elijah] looked, and behold, there was a cake baken on the coals" (1 Kings 19:6). A cake! (Confession: the translation of "cake" probably just means bread, but let's just pretend it was a cake, okay? The story is much better that way!) After he ate it, he fell asleep for one more nap before the angel woke him up again and got him going on his way.

Do you love this story? To me, the angel plays the role of the Comforter so well. On one of those days when Elijah couldn't go anymore—and for each of us that will come at different levels and at different times—when he just wanted to give up the fight and mope under a juniper tree, the Lord sent a messenger to be with him.

Sometimes you need a **lecture,**
and sometimes a **pep rally,**
but sometimes all you need is just
a **piece of cake** and a **nap.**

At times when our trials and temptations won't go away, the Comforter comes just to sit with us and refill our milk glass when it goes empty. Then, when the time is right, He will wake us up from our much-needed nap and encourage us to keep fighting the good fight.

The word *Comforter* translated in the Bible actually comes from the Latin language. *Com* means "with" and *fortis* means "strong." The word means "with strength." When the King James Bible was translated, the translators chose this word to teach that the Comforter not only comes to us to heal our wounds after battle, but also

COMES TO STAND NEXT TO US TO STRENGTHEN US DURING THOSE TIMES OF BATTLE.

I once had a dear friend who texted me from her own battle-field—she was at the hospital and didn't know what to do. Her son-in-law had been the cause of a terrible car accident with another car carrying a mom with her six young kids. Thankfully and miraculously, everyone was spared major injury, but this wasn't the first time this friend of mine had been at the hospital or jail because of the choices of her family. I think she felt like Elijah under the juniper tree. As I sat in the waiting room with her, she got a call from her own mom. As she sobbed through the story, she finally said to her mom, "Why has God abandoned our family?" I was sitting next to her, so I could overhear what her mom said next. She asked, "Who is there with you at the hospital?" She looked around at the people who had come to be there with her and listed them to her mom. Her mom simply replied, "GOD IS THERE." Her mom was teaching her that even though the Lord didn't choose to prevent all of these bad choices and the consequences that had come, and even though she was fighting a battle with her family, He would send strength to stand next to her and fight. On that day, there were

messengers sent by God that **she could see,** *and others that were standing next to her* **unseen.**

The Comforter has a divine way of giving us the ENDURANCE, POWER, and NEEDED GIFTS to get us through these hard times. Sometimes He brings peace, and other times strength. Sometimes He comes with understanding, and sometimes He just slowly mends our hearts and puts the pieces back together—one day at a time. AND SOMETIMES HE iS JUST THERE. There is a lot of peace that can come when someone just chooses to stand next to you in battle. The Comforter did not stop the gunshots when Jenny was stuck in the Garden Tomb; He just sat next to her until it was over.

There may be times, however, when we will feel quite alone during our battles and wonder if He really is there. And if He is, why isn't He doing anything? We will cry out for help, and we won't get the cake or the peace or the strength we felt we were promised. All throughout scripture there seem to be time periods when people are left alone. David was anointed as king of Israel and then sent back into the shepherd fields to wonder and wander. Moses spent forty years after leaving Egypt before the Lord came to him in the burning bush. Joseph Smith cried out in Liberty Jail in the worst months of his life—"O God, where art thou?" (Doctrine and Covenants 121:1). *Where are you!? Why did you leave me in here alone?*

> I don't know why the Spirit seems to be silent during some of these times when we need Him most. Perhaps we are just **unaware** of everything He is doing, or perhaps there is a **purpose** in His absence.

In moments like this, I try to remember two of Jesus's promises. First, the one we already saw, that He would abide in us forever (see John 14:16) That means that EVEN IF HE IS SILENT, IT DOESN'T MEAN HE DOESN'T CARE OR ISN'T THERE. And the second, a little later in that same conversation, Jesus told the disciples, "Peace I leave with you, my peace I give unto you: not as the world giveth, give I unto you. Let not your heart be troubled, neither let it be afraid" (John 14:27).

The peace of the Holy Spirit was not going to be the kind of peace the world would expect. It would come differently.

That means there will be times when we will be confused by His methods of comforting us and coming to us. Jesus told them not to *let* their heart get troubled—because they easily could. Which means trouble will still be there. And so will fear. He doesn't take those things away the way the world thinks He should. Sometimes

He ALLOWS US TO WORK THROUGH OUR PAIN. He may STAND WITH US in the battle, but He allows and perhaps WANTS US TO FIGHT and overcome so the victory is even sweeter.

Or maybe, we experience His presence like the two disciples experienced the presence of Jesus on the road to Emmaus. These two disciples were walking a road after the first Easter, and Jesus came to walk with them (this story is in Luke 24). They walked the whole way to the little city talking with Him, answering His questions, and filling Him in on what had happened the last week. These were two of Jesus's original disciples, and THEY HAD NO CLUE IT WAS HIM. After a little scripture study time and a snack, Jesus finally reveals Himself, the two disciples are shocked at who it is, and then He just as shockingly disappears. As the two of them sit in awe at the table, one of them said to the other,

"DID NOT OUR **HEART BURN WITHIN US,** WHILE HE TALKED WITH US BY THE WAY, AND WHILE HE OPENED TO US THE SCRIPTURES?" (LUKE 24:32).

It wasn't until *after* the whole experience that they were able to look back and see that He had been there with them all along. This might be the case with us too. Some hard times and some tragedies put us into an emotional daze or give us spiritual whiplash—they throw us off and make it harder for us to notice His presence. It takes a minute for us to gather ourselves again, and then we might look back and say,

"Oh—now I see. He was there all along."

So keep in mind that if you feel like you need the Spirit's companionship right now and He is not there, maybe it will TAKE SOME TIME before you are able to look back and realize that He WAS there all along. Interestingly, as the disciples walked with Jesus on the road to Emmaus, JESUS LISTENED TO THEIR TROUBLES AND THEIR CONCERNS WITHOUT SOLVING THEM. That is a powerful way to love. The Holy Spirit does this too. In the Book of Mormon, our baptismal covenants are explained as "willing to mourn with those that mourn; yea, and comfort those that stand in need of comfort, and to stand as witnesses of God at all times and in all things, and in all places" (Mosiah 18:9). Take a look at those three words—*mourn*, *comfort*, and *stand*. Wouldn't you think the Holy Spirit ministers in this same way?

SOMETIMES HE MOURNS, SOMETIMES HE COMFORTS, AND SOMETIMES HE STANDS AS A WITNESS TO WHO GOD IS.

Maybe during those times we feel left alone, what is actually happening is HE IS MOURNING WITH US. Don't you have those times when you don't want someone to make you feel better—you just want them to be sad with you? Sometimes that is what our hearts need. He knows when those times are. And He knows when to comfort us—to give advice or speak encouraging words. And He always stands as a witness of God. In all places and in all things. He will stand as a witness that God cares in a perfect way. He will not budge from that truth. He stands firm in the promise that God does not abandon. Whatever He chooses to do, He knows exactly what He is doing and why He is doing it. THERE iS A PURPOSE iN THE WAY HE COMFORTS. There is love and ministry in all of it. Looking back on previous experiences in our lives can remind us about this. We can remember the times when we knew He was there and remember how good He is. These memories can keep us from feeling like God has abandoned us or doesn't care. Because we remember that is not what He is like.

Do you remember that Enos calls moments like these a wrestle? That is such a good word for it. We have to wrestle with the different ideas of what He is like. Enos wrote in the Book of Mormon about the "wrestle which I had before God" (Enos 1:2). Please notice that the wrestle was not WITH or AGAINST God, but BEFORE Him—meaning, He was right there, a part of the battle—on our side. That is the ministry of the Spirit. And eventually, the Spirit took the truths that Enos already knew and allowed them to sink deep into his heart (see Enos 1:3).

The timing of all of this and the ways that He comforts and strengthens us do not follow a formula. He sees us as people—as friends—and MINISTERS TO US ACCORDING TO OUR OWN NEEDS. Several years after Jenny went to Jerusalem, I had my *own* chance to go there on a trip with my mom. Even though we had a house full of little kids, Jenny insisted I take the once-in-a-lifetime opportunity and enjoy the Holy Land. I wrote a little bit about this in my book *Redeemer*, but to give a little bit more to the story, toward the end of my trip, I got appendicitis while staying in these cute little huts on the shore of the Sea of Galilee. I didn't know what it was at first, but the pain started awful and then got unbearable. Eventually, my appendix burst and I was rushed down a hallway in a Jerusalem

hospital to go into emergency surgery. As they were preparing the room, they told me I should call my wife back at home to tell her goodbye—just in case. Things didn't look good for me, and they wanted to be sure she heard from me one last time before the surgery. The phone call came in the middle of the night in America and woke Jenny up. I didn't tell her how bad it possibly was, but just told her I was about to go into emergency surgery. Later on, after the trip and all the medical suspense was over, Jenny told me that the minute she heard me speak, A CALM SETTLED OVER HER AND A CONFIDENCE ENTERED HER HEART THAT EVERYTHING WAS GOING TO BE OKAY—just like it had during the riot at the tomb. Interestingly, that calm and peace didn't come to me for several days. I shared a hospital room with two other sick men, couldn't eat a thing, and have never been more miserable in all my life as my body battled to fight the infection that filled me. I even got angry with God for letting it happen and wondered what good His promises were if He wasn't going to follow through on them. I FELT ALONE DURING THOSE LONG NIGHTS—abandoned. I was probably too angry to feel the presence of or see what could've been the Spirit sitting right next to the bed with me in that room. He didn't sleep either. And He let me work through my anger. I guess I could say HE WAS MOURNING WITH ME. Several days later, after taking the sacrament out of a hospital coffee cup, a peace washed over and through me. I felt a literal surge of strength come.

There is something **significant**
and powerful to me about the timing
of the strength coming—that this happened
during the **sacrament.**

The sacrament symbols are symbols of His suffering and death. They are reminders that He walked a thorny path and experienced loneliness and was forsaken on the cross while still being loved and watched over by the Father. HE EXPERIENCED THAT COMPLETE AND TOTAL LONELINESS SO THAT WE WOULD NOT HAVE TO. I loved it when Elder Holland taught this by saying, "Because Jesus walked such a long, lonely path utterly alone, we do not have to do so. His solitary journey brought great company for our little version of that path—the merciful care of our Father in Heaven, the unfailing companionship of this Beloved Son, the consummate gift of the Holy Ghost, angels in heaven, family members on both sides of the veil, prophets and apostles, teachers, leaders, friends. All of these and more have been given as companions for our mortal journey because of the Atonement of Jesus Christ and the Restoration of His gospel. Trumpeted from the summit of Calvary is the truth that WE WILL NEVER BE LEFT ALONE NOR UNAIDED, even if sometimes we may feel that we are. Truly the Redeemer of us all said: 'I will not leave you comfortless: [My Father and] I will come to you [and abide with you].'"[19]

THE SACRAMENT IS A WEEKLY REMINDER
DURING THESE HARD TIMES THAT HE
IS STILL ON OUR SIDE.

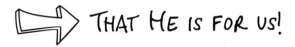 THAT HE IS FOR US!

THE HOLY GHOST STANDS AS A WITNESS
THAT WE HAVE A WOUNDED CHRIST
WHO SENDS COMFORT TO US.

That experience and witness didn't erase the struggle I was going through. The battle and wrestle in the hospital was still on, and the pain didn't go away, but for the first time I felt encouraged. Moroni taught, "BECAUSE OF MEEKNESS and LOWLINESS of heart COMETH THE VISITATION OF THE HOLY GHOST, which Comforter filleth with hope and perfect love, which love endureth by diligence unto prayer, until the end shall come, when all the saints shall dwell with God" (Moroni 8:26). That sounds like a journey verse to me—a journey the Comforter walks with us. Giving us strength in our battles *and* healing our wounds and giving hope that one day that will happen if it isn't happening today. Whether we are in riots or hospital rooms, He stays near us to give us the gifts, the company, and the exact things that we need.

THE UNCOMFORTER

A few months ago I went to a presentation of a friend of mine, and it just so happened that the audience was dotted with several people that I admire. One of those people was one of the General Presidents of one of the auxiliaries for the Church. Even though they are all just normal people, you still can't help but get a little star-struck when you see them because of how often you have seen them at general conference and on the Church website and all those fancy places (especially if you are a seminary or institute teacher!). In addition, because this particular woman had given several talks that had been so meaningful and memorable for me, it heightened my giddiness to meet her. From a distance, I watched her carry herself with such grace and dignity. IT FELT LIKE YOU WERE IN THE PRESENCE OF A QUEEN. Not the "off with their heads" type of queen, but a royal and wise leader. She was kind and confident, a gentle giant of faith, liberal with her compliments and drenched with humility. I wanted to have a chance to meet  her and tell her how much her service and speeches had meant to me. Luckily, I grew up with a mother who taught me the highest standard of manners, so I was confident I could meet her and thank her in a dignified enough way—without going too fangirl on her. I squeezed my way over to where she was, and when we met, she took my hand the way the First Lady would and looked into my eyes with fixed interest. As I introduced myself, her face lit up and she began to smile—and that's when I saw it. Right between two of her front teeth was a big old piece of green spinach. Or probably kale. She was more high-class. I was paralyzed for a minute. I didn't know what to do. What is the proper protocol for such a moment? It just took me off guard, is all. But then I went back into my typical mode and stopped her reply and said, "Sister, I am sorry but you just have a little something between your teeth that you might want to get." She quickly put her hand to her mouth and started to pick at it with the tip of her middle finger while her tongue clicked with that noise it makes in times like that. I held up my phone for her on selfie mode so she could use it as a mirror. After she was confident she got it, she looked again into the phone one last time and gave the biggest grin, turning and angling side to side a bit to be sure there weren't any other rogue plants in there, and then grabbed my arm and said, "THANK YOU! YOU ARE MY NEW BEST FRIEND!" She then turned and got mad at her other friend with her (I think the one who *used* to be her best friend) for letting her go all that time since lunch with something in her teeth.

No one actually likes being told something embarrassing about themselves or where they might be falling short or are out of line, but I WOULD RATHER HAVE THE KIND OF FRIEND WHO SPEAKS UP WHEN MY ZIPPER IS DOWN OR I NEED A MINT, or stops me when I am about to do something dumb, instead of the one who stays silent to keep the situation less awkward.

A GOOD FRIEND ALWAYS HAS YOUR BEST INTEREST IN MIND, NO MATTER WHAT YOUR REACTION IS GOING TO BE. GOOD FRIENDS ARE CANDID AND KIND AT THE SAME TIME.

They would never put their own comfort ahead of what is best for you. That is a tough friend to find and a difficult friend to be, but that is exactly THE KIND OF FRIEND YOU FIND IN THE SPIRIT. Except for with Him, it is about things way more long-lasting, meaningful, and significant than leftover lunch in your teeth.

The Holy Ghost was sent to bring comfort, peace, and reassurance to us during our journeys on the earth. That is an important mission, but He has a higher mission than just making us feel comfortable. Remember that HIS PURPOSE, along with the Father and the Son, IS TO BRING ABOUT OUR IMMORTALITY AND ETERNAL LIFE (see Moses 1:39). Eternal life is the kind of life that God lives. With all the power, wisdom, and infinite opportunity in His grasp, God chooses the type of life that brings the greatest amount of joy and fulfillment. He knows how to experience joy. He is the happiest Being in the universe. Because He also knows how to live that kind of life, the Holy Ghost seeks to guide us, persuade us, and entice us to live in the same way. Because of our freedom to choose—including the freedom to choose captivity and death—the SPIRIT SOMETIMES (and maybe often) will have to CORRECT US, LEAVE US, PUSH US, STOP US abruptly, WARN US, and DISAGREE WITH US in order to get us there.

THAT IS WHY IN ADDITION TO CALLING HIM THE **COMFORTER**, I ALSO CALL HIM THE **UNCOMFORTER**.

Peace, goose bumps, and warm fuzzies are often associated with the Holy Ghost. He is good at those. But we need to be careful if we think that is all He ever does or the only kind of feelings He gets our attention with. Take Nephi as an example. Do you remember when God commanded him to return to Jerusalem to get the brass plates? It was the Holy Ghost who inspired Lehi to send them on the three-day, scalding-hot desert trip back to the place they had just come from. That doesn't sound very peaceful, does it? Or what about when Nephi came face-to-face with a passed-out drunk Laban in the middle of the street and the Holy Ghost had to whisper, "Slay him." Do you think Nephi got warm fuzzies during *that* conversation? Let me remind you that he absolutely did not. He fought back, remember? Argued with the Spirit. "Never at any time . . ." he stammered. He shrunk back. He couldn't! The scriptures even tell us that THE SPIRIT NEEDED TO "CONSTRAIN HIM" TO FULFILL THE COMMANDMENT (see 1 Nephi 4:7–18).

When you reread or remember that story, PAY ATTENTION TO HOW GENTLE AND PATIENT THE SPIRIT WAS WITH NEPHI while asking him to do this extremely difficult and overly uncomfortable task. It was not easy for either of them, but the Holy Ghost knew where it would lead. And HE KNEW that who Nephi would become was going to BE OF FAR GREATER WORTH THAN TEMPORARILY SPARING HIM FROM SOMETHING HARD. Let's also remember, just for fun, that the Spirit was then going to tell him to put on Laban's stinky clothes, break into the treasury, lie to Laban's servant, and then tackle him when he tries to run away. Those don't give me goose bumps either.

I should probably emphasize here that the Holy Ghost will not prompt you to do things that go against the commandments of the Lord.

Notice in Nephi's story that the conversation with the Spirit is not about whether it was right or wrong to kill Laban—it was about how Nephi didn't want to. That means something was going on with the culture and law of the time that allowed for this. Kind of like a police officer or soldier in the line of duty. But just like in those situations, sometimes our duty or what we are called upon to do is extremely difficult—even when it is the right thing to do.

The HOLY GHOST IS CONSTANTLY prompting us and directing us to make decisions that will leave us feeling uncomfortable—or OUT OF OUR COMFORT ZONE. Many of you have experienced or will experience this as full-time missionaries. Leaving home, learning a new way of life or language, and talking to strangers on the street are not comfortable situations. They take courage and grit. It is important to know that

THE SPIRIT **DOES** ASK US TO DO HARD THINGS. HARD THINGS THAT BRING US CLOSER TO GOD.

I was given a ministering assignment several years ago that was super hard for me. I did not get along with the people at all. I would knock on their door and they would sometimes pretend they weren't home even though I could see them hiding behind the couch. Legit hiding! I would get so nervous on their porch—a whole colony of butterflies in my stomach. Other times I would go in and sit there on the couch while they looked at their phones, half listening to me share a message (and "half listening" is being generous). They always seemed annoyed, and every time I would leave, I would say to myself, *I am never going back there. They don't want me, and I tried.* And then the Spirit would say, PLEASE GO KNOCK AGAIN. I would say, "Why don't you knock this time?" I think He thought my sass was funny. The point is, He asks us to do tough, uncomfortable things.

{ When we think about whether a thought is coming from **Him or just us**, it cannot be based on whether we feel comfortable doing it. }

Because sometimes we might confuse uncomfortable with

wrong. SOMETIMES THE RIGHT CHOICE IS MORE UNCOMFORTABLE. (P.S. This doesn't always happen—but eventually that ministering situation turned into some of the most spiritual experiences of my life—I learned why He had pushed me out of my comfort zone.)

Not only is the Spirit willing to NUDGE US out of our COMFORT ZONES; He is also willing to DRAG US out of SINFUL ZONES. That is another area where the Holy Ghost will cause us to feel uncomfortable. Paul begged the Ephesian Saints back in the day to run away from things like greed, lust, vanity, lying, rage, and being a thief. "Neither give place to the devil. . . . And grieve not the holy Spirit of God" (Ephesians 4:27, 30). The Lord taught Joseph Smith something similar when He told him, "When we undertake to cover our sins, or to gratify our pride, . . . or to exercise control or dominion or compulsion . . . in any degree of unrighteousness, behold, the heavens withdraw themselves; the Spirit of the Lord is grieved" (Doctrine and Covenants 121:37).

There are times in our lives when our choices will grieve the Spirit.

They will make Him upset. Remember, the SPIRIT IS A PERSON, which means HE HAS EMOTIONS. He can get His heart broken. He is also able to choose when and where He would like to be. If *we* choose to be in places or to do things that He does not feel comfortable with, He will leave, and that will leave us feeling uncomfortable. I am not talking about scary or tough situations. THE HOLY GHOST IS ONE OF THE BRAVEST AND BOLDEST PEOPLE IN THE UNIVERSE. He is not scared of anyone or anything. However, He does not need to stay in a place of pornography or violence or nasty-joke telling. It might be His choice to leave, but all of His choices are motivated by love. We will feel it when the Spirit withdraws. That feeling is a signal to us that we are in a spiritually dangerous place. He doesn't give us the silent treatment to be petty or because He is offended that we chose something else over Him; He withdraws because He wants to and as a way to try to get us to come with Him.

Jenny and I once went with some friends to a fancy Broadway show. We honestly had the best seats in the house. Everyone we met that day bragged about how good the show was and how lucky we were to see it. The tickets, which our friends had given to us as a gift, were not very cheap. In fact, they flew us on a private plane, that met a limo, that took us to dinner before taking us to this show. It was a gift above all gifts. IT WAS NOT VERY MANY MINUTES INTO THE SHOW BEFORE WE KNEW THIS WASN'T THE TYPE OF PLAY WE WANTED TO BE AT. I looked over at Jenny and she was closing her eyes and covering her ears, sinking lower into her seat. I didn't know what to do. We were in the middle of the row, right in the center, and the friends who had paid for the tickets were right next to us. I didn't want to be *that guy* who made other people feel dumb, but at the same time, I did not want to stay. As I was battling through the right way to handle it, my friend bumped me with his elbow and said, "Hey, let's go." Bless up! We clumsily stepped over people with annoyed sneers and eye rolls as we walked out, but I would've walked through fire at that point to get out of that situation.

My friend's nudge was similar to times when the Holy Ghost withdraws. He never leaves without first leaning over and saying,

"Hey, let's go. This place isn't for us."

That same warning will come every time we are about to go into a place of sin. President Boyd K. Packer taught us that "no member of this Church—and that means each of you—will ever make a serious mistake without first being warned by the promptings of the Holy Ghost. . . . You may have said afterward, 'I knew I should not have done that. It did not feel right. . . .' Those impressions are the Holy Ghost attempting to direct you toward good or warning you away from harm."[20]

Even though He warns us, and we know that He is warning us, we sometimes still choose to ignore that warning. That is heartbreaking to Him. It would be to any friend. Paul and Joseph both used the word *grieve* when talking about this.

Sin grieves the Spirit.

That word is in the same family of words as *grief*. *Grief* is a funeral word. We feel grief when we lose closeness with someone—like at death. WHEN WE DELIBERATELY CHOOSE not to listen to the pleading and advice of a dear, dear friend, IT CAUSES GRIEF. For us and for Him. We lose closeness when we ignore dear friends like that. That's not how friends treat each other—especially friends who have been through so much together. Our sin—all sin—makes Him weep. Sin hurts others and ourselves, and so He feels hurt when He sees others get hurt—even and maybe especially if they bring the hurt upon themselves. But this separation does not have to be permanent. The Spirit may leave the movie theater where we are, but HE IS ANXIOUS TO BE CLOSE TO US AGAIN. HE DOES NOT LEAVE US UNCOMFORTABLE FOR HIS SAKE, BUT FOR OURS. He knows how that separation will not only grieve Him but grieve us as well. He knows how painful it is when we are apart, the guilt and consequences we experience as part of it all. I love the way King Benjamin put it when he said,

"And now, I say unto you, my brethren, that after ye have known and have been taught all these things, if ye should transgress and go contrary to that which has been spoken, that ye do withdraw yourselves from the Spirit"

(Mosiah 2:36).

I think King Benjamin places the emphasis of withdrawing on the right person. Yes, the Holy Ghost does withdraw, but the reality is, in those moments, we have actually walked away from Him.

Jesus told His disciples that when the Holy Ghost comes, "He will reprove the world of sin, and of righteousness, and of judgment" (John 16:8). *Reprove* means to convict, convince, or persuade. There are times when THE HOLY GHOST WILL DISAGREE WITH YOU. In fact, if He always thought what you are doing was right, hated the people you hate, loved the people you love, and liked all the movies, music, and jokes that you do, He would not be the Spirit. HE IS NOT AFRAID TO TELL US WE ARE WRONG OR THAT WE NEED TO CHANGE. If you were to ever ask in prayer the ways you are offending the Lord, the answer will come, and it usually comes quickly. I dare you to pray that prayer, by the way! Are you up for it?? I promise He answers. But when He reproves us of sin, He doesn't convict us or shame us because of our sin. He never says, "I can't believe you did that." He reminds us, as Jesus said, and persuades us and convicts us of our righteousness.

⭐ HE DOES NOT TELL US HE IS ASHAMED OF US; HE TELLS US WHO WE REALLY ARE. ⭐

His whisper after we sin sounds more like, *That's not you. You are a child of the Living God. You are royalty from divine courts. You are righteous and holy. You have been set free from the adversary of this world. He has no more claim on you. He is an outlaw. You don't have to listen to him. This isn't you.*

I don't know about you, but I need these kind of reminders— probably every day. Reminders of who I am and that I am lost in this world sometimes. It is too big with too many choices for a little guy like me. I need to be REMINDED that I need a Savior. I need to be

PERSUADED that sometimes the hard decisions are the ones that lead to glory. I need to be NUDGED into uncomfortable situations I wouldn't walk into on my own. And I need to be told if I have spinach in my teeth. And the Spirit—who probably prefers being the warm-fuzzies friend—is willing to take the hit, embrace the awkward, and take the silent treatment from us in order to be that kind of companion. The kind who really cares.

FOR THE DAY YOU WISH YOU WERE MORE...

≥ THE MAGNIFIER ≤

There is a legendary story in our family that gets retold at least once a year—usually at Thanksgiving dinner, and if everyone is lucky, one more time at the Christmas party. Many moons ago, one of my cousins was being a wild thing during dinner, running around making a ruckus, and my uncle kept yelling for him to knock it off. He ignored every warning and threat, and eventually the kid's chances and the dad's patience wore out. My uncle demanded that the kid go to his room right that second or he would get a paddling. When he refused one more time, my uncle stood up and they started a cat-and-mouse chase around the table until eventually my little cousin turned, stood his ground, and held out his arm, saying to his dad, "TOUCH ME NOT, for God shall smite you if ye lay your hands upon me." Everyone died laughing, and that, my friends, is the perfect way to get out of getting in trouble.

If you don't recognize that line, it comes from the story of Abinadi in the Book of Mormon. We all watched the cartoon versions of the scriptures when we were growing up, so we had all of the stories and a few lines from the scriptures memorized. It made us look smart in Primary, and apparently, those lines can also be useful if you are about to get a paddling from your pops.

Abinadi was sent on a mission to call the naughty king Noah and his people back to the love of the Lord. The great prophet-missionary was arrested and brought to the king's court for questioning in front of his priests and the two leopards that were growling at him lying next to the throne (please say you've seen that pic!). When the king ran out of patience with Abinadi's boldness, he ordered his guards to remove him from the court and put him to death. As the soldiers approached, Abinadi's face started to shine with the luster of the sun, and he called out to the guards that same line that has become dinnertime legend, "Touch me not. . . ." The story goes on and says, "After Abinadi had spoken these words . . . the people of king Noah durst not lay their hands on him, for the Spirit of the Lord was upon him" (Mosiah 13:3, 5).

In that moment, Abinadi, who was a prisoner in chains, outnumbered in the courts of his enemy, was able to hold off the king's personal guards with nothing but words.

How could that be possible?

I wonder if Ammon, another great missionary, knew this story about Abinadi. Ammon grew up with a friend named Alma. Alma's dad was there that day in the courtroom when Abinadi's face started to beam. Sometimes I like to imagine that Alma may have told his son and his buddies what it was like to hear a man like that speak. How Abinadi's words not only held off guards but CAME iNTO ALMA'S OWN HEART LiKE LiGHTNiNG.

When Ammon was called and sent on his own mission, was that story in the back of his mind? Everyone else said Ammon was crazy for wanting to go on a mission to the Lamanites. "They'll never listen," they said. "Those folks are unreachable." But maybe he knew the story of Abinadi and how his words had penetrated Alma's hardened heart. Ammon went anyway and was given sheep duty in the king's fields. You may remember that after he miraculously saved the king's sheep from thieves and robbers, Ammon was called into his own courtroom before an astonished king. When the king asked him if he was the Great Spirit (because how else could he have held off all of those sheep robbers?), Ammon replied by saying, "I am a man . . . after the image of God, and I AM CALLED BY HIS HOLY SPIRIT to teach these things . . . and a portion of that Spirit dwelleth in me, which GIVETH ME KNOWLEDGE, AND ALSO POWER" (Alma 18:34–35).

All throughout scripture, and the memories and journals of our own friends and families, there are stories of people who have done remarkable things because a portion of the Spirit was dwelling in them.

One of the great privileges of the gift of the Holy Ghost is a magnifying **power, strength,** or **ability** beyond what we are normally capable of doing.

Parley P. Pratt once taught, "The gift of the Holy Ghost . . . QUICKENS all the INTELLECTUAL FACULTIES, INCREASES, ENLARGES, EXPANDS and PURIFIES all the natural passions and affections. . . . It INSPIRES, DEVELOPS, CULTIVATES and MATURES all the fine-toned sympathies, joys, tastes, kindred feelings, and affections of our nature. It INSPIRES virtue, kindness, goodness, tenderness, gentleness, and charity. It DEVELOPS beauty of person, form and features. It TENDS to health, vigor, animation, and social feeling. It INVIGORATES all the faculties of the physical and intellectual man. It STRENGTHENS, and gives tone to the nerves. In short, it is, as it were, MARROW to the bone, JOY to the heart, LIGHT to the eyes, MUSIC to the ears, and LIFE to the whole being."[21]

You might need to read that again with a dictionary! Did you catch what that was saying?

THE GIFT OF THE HOLY GHOST ENHANCES EVERYTHING ABOUT LIFE.

All of our natural abilities are increased. Including taste. Did you see that one? I think that means strawberries can taste better because of the companionship of the Holy Ghost. And what about physical and intellectual faculties? That means sports and school. And "beauty of person, form and features"—well, that just means that like my friend Elaine Dalton likes to say, the gift of the Holy Ghost is the BEST BEAUTY SECRET that she knows about. Those who live life filled with a portion of the Spirit experience and live in a more REFINED, more VIBRANT, and more BEAUTIFUL way. It is life in 4K.

Paul describes living with the gifts of the Spirit as "a more excellent way" of living (1 Corinthians 12:31).

LIVING WITH THE GIFT OF THE HOLY GHOST ALLOWS HIM TO **INCREASE** OUR NORMAL CAPACITIES AND **INTRODUCE** **NEW** ABILITIES TO US THAT WE SIMPLY COULD NOT HAVE ON OUR OWN.

Sorry to say, this doesn't mean you can now dunk on LeBron James (unless you are already 6'6" and 260 pounds, or by the time you read this he is now a wash-up). It does mean, though, that the Spirit can MAGNIFY and HELP us with all the things we do in our lives. He happens to be an EXPERT in everything—math, the piano, languages, compassion, cooking, painting, and football.

My friend Garett is currently one of the most talented left tackles in the NFL. He is strong, smart, and resilient. Ever since he was little, he battled learning disabilities and difficult situations that made mastering anything feel like climbing Everest. During his freshman year of college, he decided he wanted to try playing football. He was tall, strong (handsome!), and grossly athletic. His one problem, though, was he couldn't learn the plays. He would study them all week, all night long, but when he got to the field, they disappeared from his mind. If he couldn't learn the plays, then the coach couldn't put him in, so it frustrated him to no end. He wanted to play so badly. One day, his mom reminded him about the promises of the companionship of the Holy Ghost. She taught him that THE SPIRIT KNEW THE PLAYS and COULD HELP HIM REMEMBER THEM—he just needed to find a way to invite the Spirit.

The next evening, Garett called his mom, over the moon in excitement. "It worked!" he yelled through the phone.

"What did??" she asked.

"I remembered my plays. Every one of them!" When his mom asked him what he had done differently, he told her he did the one thing that brought the Spirit closer to him—singing Primary songs. Particularly his favorite one, "I Am a Child of God." While the opposing punt team was out on the field, and it was almost time for Garett to go in, there he was, on the sidelines of a football game (with everything that comes with it), singing "I am a child of God, and He has sent me here. Has given me an earthly home . . ." I love picturing that moment in my mind. A 6'5", 300-pound man's man singing before he took the field. Can you even imagine what someone who overheard him must have thought? Soon, Garett realized that singing on the sidelines was tough to do in the chaos of game day, so he developed a different strategy to walk closer to the Spirit. He decided to write all over his cleats inspirational quotes and favorite scriptures so that when he looked down during the game, it would FILL HIM WITH THE SPIRIT and he would remember his plays. Even more than I love the sideline Primary program, I love picturing the opponents setting up across from him on the line and seeing scripture quotes and references written on his cleats. *Must be a softy* would just start going through their thoughts, when the ball was hiked and Garett pancaked them to the turf in 0.7 seconds.

> The Spirit cares about every aspect of our lives, and with Him as a companion, we are **more capable** than we are on our own.

Two heads are always better than one—especially if one of those heads belongs to the Holy Spirit. Although the Spirit is capable of helping us in anything—and He does!—usually, and most often, He seems to MAGNIFY THOSE THINGS THAT WE DO WHILE IN THE SERVICE OF GOD—loving and lifting other people.

There are a few spots in the scriptures where we are taught several of the different gifts that might come to us in and through the gift of the Holy Ghost to help us live and love well. Spiritual gifts are extra helps and capacities that the Holy Ghost brings to us to participate with Him in the work of the Master. Some of the spots you can find the gifts in scripture are 1 Corinthians 12, Romans 12, Moroni 10, and Doctrine and Covenants 46. Each of these chapters includes lists of spiritual gifts that the Lord gives to us through the Holy Spirit to bless and strengthen the lives of other people. As you look through the lists of gifts, which include gifts like the gift to KNOW, the gift to administer MERCY, the gift of WISDOM, the gift to HEAL, the gift to perform MIRACULOUS ACTS, and the gift of TONGUES, you may notice some that you have seen in yourself or your close friends and family members. Remember as you look at the lists that these are not the only gifts and ways that the Spirit strengthens or empowers people to do the work God has called them to do. Some others we might add to those lists would include the gift to be PATIENT with others, the gift of ENTHUSIASM for life, the gift to LAUGH, the gift to LISTEN, the gift of CREATIVITY, the gift of being LOYAL, or the gift of LOVING OTHERS well.

"AND ALL THESE GIFTS COME **FROM GOD,** FOR THE BENEFIT OF THE CHILDREN OF GOD"
(DOCTRINE AND COVENANTS 46:26).

There are a million-plus different gifts and ways that the Spirit can magnify how we are living. You might be thinking right now about your spiritual gifts—or maybe even wondering if you have any. YOU DO! It just might be hard to admit or see in yourself. Have you ever been in a job interview when someone asks you about some of your good qualities? That is an impossible question for me to answer. I always feel so awkward saying what I think I am good at. One time I was so flustered by the question I literally answered like this, "Well, I am just a great person to be around." What?! Who says that? I actually asked the interview lady if I could start over. I didn't get the job. It might feel similar with acknowledging spiritual gifts. However, this should help.

SPIRITUAL GIFTS AREN'T ABOUT US. They didn't come to us because of our unique abilities or hard work. GIFTS ARE GIFTS. They come to us from someone else. We don't brag about what was in our stocking on Christmas morning. That's called gratitude—not bragging. It is okay to recognize and realize and be thankful that God trusts us with certain gifts. They always COME TO US TO BLESS AND LIFT AND HELP THE LIFE OF SOMEONE ELSE. THEY ARE NOT ABOUT US. Having said that, you still might be wondering what your gift might be. Some of your gifts might be mentioned in your patriarchal blessing if you have one. Or you might want to ask your parents, leaders, or close friends what they see in you. One of my favorite experiences as a bishop was at girls' camp one year when I felt prompted to look around the campfire and tell each of the girls a spiritual gift I saw in each of them. That was a gift in and of itself, by the way—the ability to see a gift in another person I didn't know super well.

As we go throughout life, the Holy Spirit will bring **different gifts** to us **as we need them** to make the world **a better place.**

And remember that none of the gifts are greater than another. No one is more special or more needed because of a particular gift. Every football team has left tackles and corners. Every baseball team needs a catcher and a pitcher. Everybody needs an ear and a foot. Remember—it isn't about us as individuals; it is about us as the family of God. THE GIFTS ARE GIVEN SO THAT WE CAN ALL LIFT EACH OTHER.

Tonight, the night I am writing this chapter, a friend of mine is packing his last few things into his suitcase getting ready to leave for a full-time mission. He is excited, but nervous and not very confident. As a teacher at the MTC, seminary/institute teacher, and bishop, I saw this literally hundreds of times with missionaries. They pack their bags with hesitation—wondering if they can do this or not—and sometime soon after they make it through the doors of the MTC, the Holy Spirit pours out an endowment of encouragement on them and they light up inside with confidence, faith, and hope. It isn't about them. The gifts are God working through them to do His magnificent work.

I love when Peter says about Jesus, "How God anointed Jesus of Nazareth with the Holy Ghost and with power: who went about doing good, and healing all that were oppressed of the devil; for God was with him" (Acts 10:38). JESUS WAS GIVEN the POWER that comes THROUGH THE HOLY SPIRIT to do the great and marvelous works that He did while He was on the earth. YOU TOO WERE GIVEN that same gift of the HOLY SPIRIT—power to do good and heal those who are oppressed because that same God is with you. Interestingly, Peter, the one who was saying that about Jesus, experienced this first-hand. Peter started out as a humble lakeside fisherman. He was young, inexperienced, and rough around the edges. The night Jesus was taken away by guards, Peter didn't even have the guts to tell a teenage girl that he knew who Jesus was (see Matthew 26:69). He denied Him two other times that very night. That same Peter, on the day of Pentecost, when the Holy Ghost came down upon them "and they were all filled" (Acts 2:4), stood up with others and testified about Jesus in different languages with such boldness and courage the people standing around thought they were drunk (see Acts 2:13). THEY COULDN'T BELIEVE THAT A MAN FROM GALILEE—A COUNTRY BUMPKIN FISHERMAN—COULD SPEAK AND PREACH WITH SUCH POWER. At the end of Peter and the other disciples' testimony meeting, 3,000 people asked to be baptized to change and follow Jesus.

>> Once Peter had the magnifying power of the Holy Spirit, he was unstoppable. <<

Several years ago, I was called to be a bishop in our ward and was completely overwhelmed. I had the same feeling that day as the day I went into the MTC. *I can't do this*, I thought. *I can't represent the Lord*. When my stake president extended the call, I just sat there and cried. The first words out of my mouth were, "But I am just a kid." I don't remember much more of the conversation, except that Jenny handled it with all the grace of heaven and said, "Well, we will just use this opportunity to come closer to God." (That girl!) Not long after that interview, I came across a scripture I loved in the Book of Mormon. It is actually in the book called Words of Mormon. It is in the spot where he is explaining to future readers how and why the Book of Mormon got put together the way it did. You see, when Mormon was younger—just a kid—the Lord led him to a cave full of records—piles of plates that had a thousand-year history of the Nephites and Lamanites. There, He asked Mormon to go through all of those records and pick out the parts we would need in the future. These selections would later become the Book of Mormon as we have it today. Mormon walked into the room SURROUNDED BY MOUNTAINS OF RECORDS and had to CHOOSE AND SUMMARIZE and compile a set of plates that millions of people would look to for strength, testimony, and HELP THROUGH THEIR LIVES 1,400 YEARS AFTER HE LIVED. I cannot imagine how overwhelmed he felt. But this is what he said:

"I DO THIS FOR A WISE PURPOSE; FOR THUS **IT WHISPERETH ME,** ACCORDING TO THE **WORKINGS OF THE SPIRIT** OF THE LORD WHICH IS IN ME. AND NOW, I DO NOT KNOW ALL THINGS; BUT THE LORD KNOWETH ALL THINGS WHICH ARE TO COME; WHEREFORE, HE WORKETH IN ME TO DO ACCORDING TO HIS WILL"
(WORDS OF MORMON 1:7).

HOW DID MORMON KNOW which verses to include and which parts to summarize? THE SPIRIT WHISPERED them to Him and worked through Him to put together what we now know as the Book of Mormon. I think he did a pretty good job, don't you? That verse explaining that gave me great strength then, and it still does today. I DON'T KNOW ALL THINGS—and I certainly can't do all things—BUT GOD DOES and can.

And THE HOLY SPIRIT CAN WORK IN ME and through me to accomplish amazing things.

I had one of those times when that happened. It wasn't as a bishop, but just as a friend. As I was walking along just talking about this and that with a good friend of mine, the Spirit whispered something to me to say to him. I could sense that something was going on with him—that he was struggling on the inside. But you couldn't tell from the conversation. It was just a happy, funny, normal chat. But I said what I thought the Lord wanted me to say. Immediately his eyes filled up with tears and he said to me, "How did you know?"

I said,

"I didn't. But the Spirit did. And what that means, is there is a God in heaven who adores you and is anxious for you to know that."

On that day, in that random spot on the stairs, the Spirit poured extra compassion and intuition into my heart and worked in me to know something I couldn't have ever known on my own, and then for and in behalf of Him, I was able to wrap up that kid in a big bear hug.

The Spirit is able to MAKE US MORE THAN WE ARE. He is able to reach people through us that we couldn't ever reach on our own. He is able to give us courage that we thought we never had. To love in a way we didn't know our hearts could. The Spirit strengthens us to endure hard things that otherwise would've crushed us. HE OPENS UP

THE WAY FOR US TO LIVE HAPPIER, HOLIER, HEALTHIER LIVES. We may feel like we are not enough—no, we may *know* that we are not enough—but with the Holy Spirit, we can say for ourselves Paul's words:

"I can do all things through Christ which strengtheneth me" (Philippians 4:13).

That strength comes as a gift of grace through the presence and power of the Holy Spirit. And just like with Abinadi, that same fire, passion, and power that raised Jesus from the grave lives in us (see Romans 8:10).

For the Day You Want to Know How . . .

RECEIVING THE HOLY GHOST

I rarely mention this publicly, but I legitimately cry every time I walk down Main Street in Disneyland. I also cry when I buy tickets for eight people to walk down Main Street in Disneyland—but that is for another reason. There is something about all the people there with the anticipation of magic and memories that mixes up real good deep down in me. Our favorite people to go to Disneyland with are my aunt, uncle, and cousins the Bunkers. They have the same passion for the place, and my cousin Kasey is my only rival in Disney trivia. She gets close every time. They know all the secrets of the park—how and when to get fast passes, the quickest routes, the "cheapest" burgers—all the things. We went with them one time during a huge anniversary celebration of something. I don't remember what it was for, but I remember they were handing out special passes every morning to random people. THE PASSES GAVE YOU UNLIMITED ACCESS TO THE FRONT OF EVERY LINE IN THE PARK. One of my cousins heard from some folks at the hotel the night before our last day that if you were by a certain trash can in Fantasyland at a certain time, a worker would come out of a certain door and you could snag the passes. We got up extra early and like a bunch of vultures we circled the trash can until we saw the worker come out with passes in hand and wouldn't you know—boom! We got them! That day is the funnest day I have ever spent at Disneyland. Right to the front of every line—flashing my pass like I owned the ride. VIPs. All summer long, we had heard that the magic passes were handed out to random guests somewhere in the park. However, once we learned that there was a schedule to the randomness, AS LONG AS WE WERE IN THE RIGHT PLACE, AT THE RIGHT TIME, DOING THE RIGHT THING, WE COULD GET THE PASSES.

This is true of receivers in football, too. They don't magically catch the ball. They have a route, and they have to juke out the defender and they have to be in the right place at the right time doing the right thing in order to receive the ball. It's hardly random. If they are listening, the quarterback will yell out his "Blue 42" or some other code phrase that tells the receiver where and when to go to receive.

When we are baptized as members of the restored Church of Jesus Christ, we are then eligible to receive the gift of the Holy Ghost. If we choose to participate in that ordinance, then Melchizedek Priesthood holders set their hands on our heads, and after confirming us a member of the Church, they say these words:

"Receive the Holy Ghost."

And just like magic tickets and touchdown completions, this does not happen randomly. THESE WORDS in the ordinance ARE ADVICE AND INSTRUCTION to *us* to receive, NOT A COMMAND for heaven to send. Throughout this book, we have been talking about the privileges and gifts that can flow into our lives because of the companionship of the Holy Spirit. At this point, I hope you are saying—*I am convinced! Sign me up! Now teach me how to receive and live life in this more excellent way.*

The first thing we want to remember, again, is that the Holy Ghost is a living soul and is not forced to do anything. We want to be careful NOT TO MAKE A FORMULA for how to receive the Spirit like it is a password to open some treasure box. Do you remember that conversation between Jesus and Nicodemus we talked about earlier? Remember, the one where Nicodemus wanted to climb back into his mother to be born again? Bless his heart one more time. During that conversation, the Lord made a comparison between the Spirit and the wind: "The wind bloweth where it listeth, and thou hearest the sound thereof, but canst not tell whence it cometh, and whither it goeth: so is every one that is born of the Spirit" (John 3:8). In modern English, what that means is no one knows where the wind comes from. It just shows up and then blows through, off to somewhere else. You can't follow it when it leaves and you can't force it to come. That is what the Spirit is like. He comes and goes according to His infinite wisdom and love. We cannot demand Him to come or force His help.

THE WAY WE LIVE IS NOT A FORMULA, BUT INSTEAD A DESIRE TO BE CLOSE WITH HIM.

The Lord has taught us, though, principles that can help us come closer and live with more of His influence in our lives.

Let's start with the principle of asking.

THAT IS LESSON
NUMBER ONE—TO **RECEIVE** ←
THE HOLY SPIRIT IN MORE
ABUNDANCE, WE **PLEAD**
→ **TO GOD** FOR MORE
OF HIS INFLUENCE
AND POWER.

Growing up, I was always afraid to ask my parents if I could do something, because I didn't want to be disappointed with a no. I was so nervous about it that sometimes I would lie to my friends and tell them that I had extra chores to do or something because I couldn't handle actually asking and then being let down. Amazingly, EVERY TIME I DIDN'T ASK, I DIDN'T GET TO GO. The Lord's most repeated principle throughout all of scripture is so simple:

"Ask, and ye shall receive"
(D&C 4:7).

"For EVERY ONE THAT ASKETH RECEIVETH; and HE THAT SEEKETH FINDETH; and to him that KNOCKETH IT SHALL BE OPENED." You have probably heard those verses before, but I love the next verses (the ones that go with it) even more. "If a son shall ask bread of any of you that is a father, will he give him a stone? or if he ask a fish, will he for a fish give him a serpent?" (Luke 11:10–11). But what if? Can you imagine a kid asking his parents for a PB&J and getting a rock instead? IMPERFECT PARENTS KNOW HOW TO GIVE REALLY GREAT GIFTS TO THEIR CHILDREN, which means GOD, the most perfect parent of all, KNOWS HOW TO GIVE PERFECT GIFTS. "How much more shall your heavenly Father give the Holy Spirit to them that ask him?" (Luke 11:13). It is so simple that sometimes it is overlooked. We might think,

if God already knows that we want it, then **why** does He wait for us to ask?

It might be because God wants to be a dad, and not a vending machine. He wants a conversation—to hear our dreams, hopes, desires, pleads. And He wants the Spirit to be a lifelong companion, and not the bag of chips at B3. Asking and desiring is all about relationship.

I love the story of the little tax collector named Zacchaeus. One day when Jesus was coming through his neck of the woods, Zacchaeus wanted to see Him, but "could not for the press" (Luke 19:3). Luke was talking about the crowd that surrounded Jesus, but

I love the description of the word, "the press." It was the press that kept Zacchaeus from seeing Jesus. HOW MANY THINGS DO YOU AND I HAVE PRESSING INTO OUR MINDS, LIVES, AND SCHEDULES RIGHT NOW? A recent *USA Today* article said that most Americans claim to be busier this year than they were last year, and busier last year than they were the year before.[22] Life is crazy busy. School, soccer practice, piano lessons, homework, chores, school, church stuff, choir, football, play practice, and school. We rarely have any time to ourselves. And some of the time we do have—that we haven't already given away— we give to our phones or to Fortnite. Have you ever checked how much time you spend on certain apps? It is shocking. You might not want to see it and face the reality. Sadly, my phone is usually the last thing I see before I go to bed and the first thing I see in the morning. There is just a lot of stuff going on. The press is real, and just like it kept Zacchaeus from seeing Jesus, it can keep us from receiving the influence and power of the Holy Ghost. Last night, when I was praying, I actually *said* to Heavenly Father, "I am not sure what I need to do next in my life right now. I am so confused. I just need help and a nudge in the right direction, but I am too tired right now to listen for an answer." True story! I know what it takes to hear the Spirit, so now it is just a matter of asking how badly I want to. In Zacchaeus's story, HE WANTED TO SEE JESUS SO BAD THAT HE CLIMBED A TREE. Maybe we need to do the same in our lives. Find a tree to climb every now and then—it doesn't have to be a real tree (but it can be!), but a place you can go to escape the press to enjoy more of the peaceful power that comes from the presence of the Spirit. Maybe it is up in the mountains or down at the beach for you. For some it might be a quiet minute before bedtime, or sitting in the truck in the driveway after school (that was mine!). Right place . . . right time . . . doing the right thing.

THIS IS GOING TO BE PRINCIPLE NUMBER TWO— FIND A TREE TO CLIMB, A PLACE WHERE →YOU CAN HEAR HIS VOICE AND SIT IN HIS INFLUENCE.←

Listen, if the Spirit wants to talk to us, He can. He could push the press out of the way, and He can talk louder than your phone. When He wanted to get people's attention in the scriptures, He spoke through donkeys, rocks, and out of the clouds. He can walk through doors and walls. If He wants to speak, He can speak. But usually, like a gentleman, He waits for us to be listening. No one likes talking to people when they are staring at their phones and not at them. I don't think He would like it either. It's not that He can't; He just usually doesn't.

SOMETIMES BEING IN THE RIGHT PLACE HELPS US RECEIVE THE SPIRIT. A certain setting can tune our hearts to the right channel. I came home one day and Jenny was doing something in the kitchen, so I asked what she was up to and she answered back, "Baking cookies."

I wasn't trying to be a brat, but I thought about it for a minute and said back, "Well, actually, *you* aren't baking the cookies; the oven is." I didn't get a cookie that day, but I have thought about that in relationship to the Spirit. It really is the oven that turns dough into cookies. Jenny doesn't have enough hot breath to turn flour, water, eggs, and chocolate chips into cookies. It takes a power greater than what she has. What Jenny *can* do, and does do so wonderfully well, darling, is put the dough in the right place. Out on the counter, nothing would ever happen (except me eating the dough)—it is only in the oven that the power can be felt and have an effect.

PUTTING OURSELVES IN PLACES WHERE THE SPIRIT COMES MORE NATURALLY IS PRINCIPLE NUMBER THREE.

I remember sitting in church as a young teenager during fast and testimony meeting. For people who visit our churches, that can be a wild experience—you never know what people are going to say. On this particular day, one of my spiritual heroes, Calvin Griffin, stood up to bear his testimony. Calvin had a heart that was as large as his biceps. He looked like he could dunk on anyone in the ward. He was tall, strong, hilarious, and sweet. When he spoke, he had a little bit of a stutter on some of his letters. I was sitting in my pew, folding up my program into fake origami, when Calvin started talking. Immediately I was captured when he said, "I b-b-b-believe in God the Eternal Father!" THAT TESTiMONY WENT iNTO MY HEART LiKE LiGHTNiNG. It was so unexpected. It just came with unsuspecting force. IT BECAME A FOUNDATiONAL PART OF MY OWN TESTiMONY. I have been to lots of testimony meetings since then. Sometimes they are powerful and sometimes they are not.

Again, we don't get to decide which places the Spirit is going to come with more power and force, but there are some places and situations where the potential for His influence is higher and can be stronger.

We can PUT OURSELVES THERE—like cookies in the oven—in holy places. Places that have a higher likelihood of inviting the Spirit.

President Henry B. Eyring once taught, "If you have felt the influence of the Holy Ghost during this day . . . you may take it as evidence that the Atonement is working in your life. For that reason and many others, you would do well to put yourself in places and in tasks that invite the prompting of the Holy Ghost."[23] As a really important side note, if I used the scriptures and the stories of Jesus as a guide to the right kinds of places and the right kinds of tasks that invite the prompting of the Holy Ghost, I think I WOULD FIND MYSELF NEAR THE LONELY, THE OUTCAST, THE REJECTED, AND THE FRIENDLESS, and I think I WOULD FIND MYSELF IN TASKS LIKE LIFTING, LOVING, AND LEARNING TO BE LIKE HIM. That's where He always was—seems like the Spirit would choose the same.

Another way we can increase our ability to receive the Holy Ghost is to repent often. The effects and influence of sin and other strong emotions can be so loud in our lives. They can drown out the influence of the Holy Ghost. Elder Richard G. Scott once taught, "The Holy Spirit can be overcome or masked by strong emotions, such as anger, hate, passion, fear, or pride. When such influences are present, it is like trying to savor the delicate flavor of a grape while eating a jalapeno pepper. Both flavors are present, but one completely overpowers the other."[24] I remember trying this out after I heard Elder Scott's talk. Give it a go if you want—but you probably don't need to in order to believe him.

((Repenting often gives us a peace of mind and quiet conscience that allows us to hear more clearly.))

When someone like Elder Scott teaches this, he is not threatening that the Holy Ghost will leave, or saying, "You better get rid of these other influences or else!" He is trying to teach from his experience what has helped him hear and be under the guidance and influence of the Holy Ghost better. That is the whole purpose of the *For the Strength of Youth* booklet. HAVE YOU EVER GONE THROUGH AND LOOKED FOR THE "WHY" IN EVERY CHAPTER INSTEAD OF THE "WHAT"? The chapters are not meant to explain how to be a good Christian by telling us what the rules are, but rather each page of that book is a guide to help us enjoy the presence of the Spirit.

The Holy Ghost is always trying to be with us. He is not looking for ways to leave or be extra sensitive.

He enjoys our presence **as much** as we enjoy His.

Maybe even more. Well, there is no maybe about it. He is willing and ready and anxious to be a close part of our lives. I don't know if you have ever seen an old-school radio before, but they had this knob on them that would tune the radio to certain frequencies. Once the radio was on the right sound frequency (please don't ask me what that means), you would hear music or sports radio. The crazy thing is that particular song or speech or commercial you all of a sudden hear was already flying through the air. In fact, all around you there is music playing in the air, but you can only hear it when you tune a radio to the right channel. Each of you has found or will find different choices you can make or things you can do that tune your heart to recognize and come closer to the Spirit. We cannot force Him, but He isn't random. We just need to put ourselves in those right places, at the right times, doing the things that turn the knob on our hearts. Whether it is scriptures on our shoes or finding our tree to climb, we find a way to walk closer with Him and ask Him to be a bigger part of our lives. And when we ask, we receive His presence—a gift better than VIP passes, overtime touchdowns, or some of Jenny's chocolate chip cookies.

CONCLUSION

One of the bonuses of getting married is all the gifts that you get. After all the dancing and the cake and the honeymoon, you get to come back to loads and loads of presents. It is like a birthday times seventeen. You get some crazy stuff, stuff you never use, multiples of some things (we got fourteen waffle makers—fourteen! I must look like I like waffles), and stuff you put away in a closet to wrap up later and give to someone else at *their* wedding. Those are called regifts. There is probably a crystal vase that has been passed around weddings for years around these parts. One of the gifts Jenny and I got was this blue and white and yellow quilt. I may have snarled my face when I saw it for the first time. I mean, it was nice, but it looked like it belonged in my great-aunt's guest bedroom. And who gives a blanket as a gift?

I think it is one of those fancy quilts—you know, the ones that you buy and never use? I grew up with those. My mom is an interior designer and is so good at what she does. People even pay her to come decorate their Christmas trees. But growing up in the house of an interior designer meant that half of the house was breakable and the other half was only for looks. WE HAD SO MANY THINGS IN THE HOUSE THAT MY MOM SAID WE COULDN'T TOUCH OR USE. We had a whole staircase we weren't even allowed to use. We called it the *Beauty and the Beast* staircase because it was fancy like the one from the movie. The one *we* could use we called the Cinderella one—for the peasant children. But back to the blankets. All of our beds had these comforters and big fluffy pillows that we weren't allowed to use either. THEY WERE ONLY THERE FOR SHOW. But they were so comfy! Because of the way I was raised, that blue, white, and yellow blanket sat on the edge of our bed for a while until one day I abandoned the rules of my youth and gave it a try. I wish you could see it today. It is wasted and worn out. There are frayed edges, holes in the middle, and a whole lot of memories. That blanket goes everywhere with me, and I refuse to sleep without it. What a shame it would be if I had never taken it off the edge of the bed.

I like that the Holy Ghost and that kind of blanket share a nickname—the Comforter—or in Greek, the Helper—because sometimes I feel like SOME OF US TREAT THE GIFT OF THE HOLY GHOST JUST LIKE THOSE FANCY BLANKETS. THEY ARE THERE, BUT THEY ONLY SIT THERE FOR SHOW— and are never enjoyed. The difference, of course, is that the Holy Ghost is not a blanket; He is a person. And just like the Father and the Son, He happens to be one of the kindest, sweetest, most dynamic, interesting, powerful people in the whole universe. Someone way out of our league, but anxious for friendship and fellowship with us. He has the best advice, and wants to give it. He is the most courageous companion and wants to stand near. He is the most optimistic encourager and seeks to tell us what He sees in us every day.

He is the world's **best gift giver.** His gifts are always perfect, thoughtful, and exactly what we always wanted **even when we didn't know** we needed them.

He knows how to lead us, correct us, and help us become better versions of ourselves than we ever knew we could be. But for so many, He sits quietly, close by, cheering in silence, and waiting for a chance to give more.

When Jesus was about to leave the world, He reminded the disciples that "John truly baptized with water; but ye shall be baptized with the Holy Ghost not many days hence" (Acts 1:5). WHEN JOHN BAPTIZED WITH WATER IT WAS BY IMMERSION—completely covered in the water. That is the SAME TYPE OF BAPTISM THAT JESUS WAS HOPING THE DISCIPLES WOULD EXPERIENCE WITH THE HOLY GHOST. All the way immersed in His goodness, power, and presence. Not sprinkled. Not just a toe in, but our WHOLE SELVES, for our whole lives.

Remember in the beginning of the book I told you I was a movie guy? Well, if there were a book of the Bible I wish they would make a movie of, it would be the book of Judges. No one ever reads it because it is named the book of Judges, but it has some stories in it to tell! A long-haired man who tears lions apart, an evil king so fat a knife gets lost in his belly, and a woman who saves a nation by driving a stake through the captain of the enemy army. We aren't sure what it would be rated, but it would sell tickets. The real magic in the book of Judges is how it is everyone's story. Those examples didn't sound like everyday stories, but

the theme of the book over and over again is **people getting themselves into trouble,** turning to the Lord for help, and the Lord **sending someone to be a hero.**

Best-picture kind of stuff. One of my favorite stories in the book of Judges is of a woman named Deborah. During the days of Deborah, the tribes of Israel were in slavery once again to a neighboring conquering nation named the Canaanites. The author of Judges introduces Deborah like this: "Deborah, a prophetess, the wife of Lapidoth, . . . dwelt under the palm tree . . . and the children of Israel came up to her for judgment" (Judges 4:4–5). Can you already tell you are going to like her? A prophetess is a woman who has the gift of prophecy. The gift of prophecy in scripture is the gift to speak hope and see goodness in the future of others. It is also a gift of having the testimony of Jesus. People would come from all over to her favorite palm tree and they would get advice and counsel and encouragement from her. I adore that she chose a palm tree—my kind of girl! I left the phrase "wife of Lapidoth" in there because in the original Hebrew Bible it can be translated differently. The other option is "woman of a torch-like spirit."[25] We don't know who thought translating it as "wife of Lapidoth" would be a good idea, but I prefer the other one. A WOMAN WITH A TORCH-LIKE SPIRIT, who LIGHTS UP OTHERS' souls with HOPE, COUNSEL, and the TESTIMONY OF JESUS. We all need a Deborah! When the children of Israel started pleading with the Lord for help to escape their enemies, the Lord selected a battle captain named Barak to lead out the Israelite army. Israel was outnumbered big-time, and it gave Barak the willies to think about going to fight against the Canaanite army. He couldn't do it! They were too big! And God called the wrong guy! With knees knocking, he went to see Deborah, and this is what he said (it is your favorite part!): "If thou wilt go with me, then I will go: but if thou wilt not . . . , then I will not" (Judges 4:8).

Even though Deborah doesn't speak in this verse, it is my favorite verse about her. There was something about Deborah—her courage, her wisdom, her torch-like spirit—that made her THE KIND OF PERSON WHO GIVES STRENGTH, POWER, AND ENCOURAGEMENT TO OTHERS WHEN SHE IS NEAR. If she came, Barak would willingly go against the enemy terribly outnumbered. Her presence would give him the courage to move and to fight and to win.

We don't know very much at all about the premortal world. But I can imagine myself standing under a palm tree in heaven right on the edge of coming into this wild, wild world, terribly outnumbered, and saying to the Spirit—

IF THOU WILT GO WITH ME, THEN I WILL GO.

Because I knew there would be days when I would need His help connecting with heaven from behind the veil, and days of worry and wonder when His burning confirmations would be needed. I knew I would need His guidance for days I was lost and would need His correction and His cleansing touch for days I fell short. I knew on days of commotion and weakness I would need His strength and His peace. I once had a Sunday School teacher say that after our lives we could watch them on a big movie screen in the sky. I am not sure if that is true, but if you saw it, you would know I was right—I have had and continue to have plenty of these types of days. And He has always been there.

When Nephi had his conversation with the Spirit, he said he was "caught away . . . into an exceedingly high mountain, which I never had before seen, and upon which I never had before set my foot" (1 Nephi 11:1). Within minutes, He is seeing things He has never seen, understanding truths He never knew, and praising and believing in Jesus in ways he never had before.

XOXOXOXO XOXOXOXO XOXOXOXO XOXOXOXO XOXOXOXO XOX

This is the kind of life you and I can expect when we walk it side by side with the Holy Spirit. He will take us to those places we have never been before—places we didn't even know we could go.

XOXOXOXO XOXOXOXO XOXOXOXO XOXOXOXO XOXOXOXO XOX

Those are the marks of a life lived immersed in the friendship of the Spirit. And He really is the perfect friend.

There is a friend I have now that I once texted and said, "Isn't it amazing that of all the people in the world, and all the ages of time, you and I happened to be put in the same place, at the same time, with the chance to do life together? We will always have that bond with each other." That is a bond I hope I can say I shared with the Spirit as well.

Of all the gifts that He gives, let's **never forget** that the greatest of all of them was a chance to live life **side by side** with the **Giver Himself.**

And if they really do play a big movie in the sky of our lives on earth, you and I can find some big beanbag chairs up there, and I'll grab my worn-out comforter, and as we watch I will show you all the parts and times when I did what I did, and said what I said, and believed what I believed, and lived how I lived, all because He agreed to come with me.

NOTES

1. Russell M. Nelson, "Revelation for the Church, Revelation for Our Lives," *Ensign*, May 2018.

2. Neal A. Maxwell, *The Promise of Discipleship* (Salt Lake City: Deseret Book, 2001), 92–93.

3. Neil L. Andersen, "A Compensatory Spiritual Power for the Righteous," Brigham Young University devotional, August 18, 2015.

4. *Teachings of Presidents of the Church: Joseph Smith* (2011), 43.

5. Andrew F. Ehat and Lyndon W. Cook, eds., *The Words of Joseph Smith: The Contemporary Accounts of the Nauvoo Discourses of the Prophet Joseph* (Orem, Utah: Grandin Book Company, 1996), 382.

6. Jeffrey R. Holland, in "Learning about the Godhead," https://www.churchof jesuschrist.org/youth/article/learning-about-the-godhead.

7. Heber C. Kimball, in *Journal of Discourses*, 4:222.

8. Joseph Fielding Smith, *Doctrines of Salvation,* comp. Bruce R. McConkie, 3 vols. (1954–56), 1:38.

9. Boyd K. Packer, "The Twenty-Mark Note," BYU–Idaho devotional, March 12, 2002.

10. David A. Bednar, Face to Face event, May 12, 2015, https://www.churchof jesuschrist.org/broadcasts/face-to-face/elder-and-sister-bednar.

11. Dallin H. Oaks, "Teaching and Learning by the Spirit," *Ensign*, March 1997.

12. Ronald A. Rasband, "Let the Holy Spirit Guide," *Ensign*, May 2017.

13. See https://www.history.com/news/buzz-aldrin-communion-apollo-11-nasa.

14. Joseph Fielding Smith, "The First Presidency and the Council of the Twelve," *Improvement Era* 69:979.

15. David A. Bednar, "Always Retain a Remission of Your Sins," *Ensign*, May 2016.

16. D. Todd Christofferson, "The Power of Covenants," *Ensign*, May 2009.

17. Joseph B. Wirthlin, "Windows of Light and Truth," *Ensign*, November 1995.

18. See https://www.churchofjesuschrist.org/prophets-and-apostles/unto-all-the -world/spirit-can-guide-all-aspects-of-life-elder-scott-says?lang=eng.

19. Jeffrey R. Holland, "None Were with Him," *Ensign*, May 2009.

20. Boyd K. Packer, "How to Survive in Enemy Territory," Seminary Centennial Broadcast, January 22, 2012.

21. Parley P. Pratt, *Key to the Science of Theology*, 9th ed. (1965), 101.
22. See https://www.psychologytoday.com/us/blog/the-time-cure/201302/hurry-sickness.
23. Henry B. Eyring, "Gifts of the Spirit for Hard Times," Brigham Young University devotional, September 10, 2006.
24. Richard G. Scott, "To Acquire Spiritual Guidance," *Ensign*, November 2009.
25. Alfred Edersheim, *The Bible History: Old Testament* (1995), 121.

ABOUT THE AUTHOR

DAVID BUTLER is by day a religious educator sharing his fierce love for the scriptures with anyone willing to listen. By night he is a fort builder, waffle maker, sports coach, and storyteller for his six darling kids. Somewhere in between, he is a motivational speaker and writer. He loves, loves, loves good food, spontaneous adventures, Christmas morning, the first day of summer, and every other day of summer. Above all he loves people. He has chosen as his life motto, "Stuff no mattah. People mattah." He and his adorable wife, Jenny, live with their family amid the snowcapped peaks of the Mountain West, but they often dream of a beach house on a sunny shore somewhere.

 @mrdavebutler